GREEK COOKERY
from the HELLENIC HEART

GREEK COOKERY
from the HELLENIC HEART

GEORGE CALOMBARIS

PHOTOGRAPHY DEAN CAMBRAY

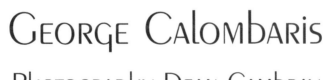

NEW
HOLLAND

Efharisto—thank you

What makes a person successful are the people who surround them—those with the same ethics, a family approach to life, full of love, humility and passion; never judgemental, but always supportive. I have been very blessed to have all these people around me.

Firstly to my mum. Thank you for giving me a palate and an understanding of the soul in cooking and thank you for sharing your recipes that represent us to the world.

Dad. Thank you for always being my rock and giving me morals that made me into the man I am today. You're a legend mate!

To my brother Nick and sister Nicole; I love you both and thank you for giving me the most beautiful god-children, nieces and nephews: Michael, Iliana, Anthea and Michael.

My Yia Yia Mahi not only feeds me the most refined Greek Cypriot food when I visit her, she also feeds me her love and the history of our family and her country. She gives me a sense of pride in my family values and what they represent to me—a proud Australian but a very passionate Greek Cypriot!

They say behind every man... I say I have a Natalie. Supportive, understanding, strong and beautiful. Thank you Natalie X.

Thank you to the people who represent me every day and fly the flag: Angie Giannakodakis my restaurant manager, Justin Wise and Travis McAuley my head chefs, Lauren Calleja, Andrew Phillpot, Maria Klinakis, Spiro Vrakas, Sam Maher, Malcolm Singh, Olivia Hardie, Natasha McAuley, Colette Ruiters, Nick Daglis and Katerina Nestorovska. And of course the rest of the 120 staff including kitchen hands, waiters and waitresses, chefs and office staff who work at The Press Club, Hellenic Republic, Maha and The Belvedere Club. You all rock!

A big thanks to all my partners Shane Delia, George Sykiotis, Tony Lachimea, Joe Calleja and my associates in Greece, Tasos and Nikolas Ioannidis. Thank you for believing in me and never doubting my madness!

To all my suppliers and affiliates who support the madness THANK YOU!

A very special thank you to Dean Cambray for, again, bringing my vision to paper. Thanks Deano!

George Calombaris
Agapi and Filakia

A battle will occur for the freedom of Cyprus,
with the hope of being united to the diamond
which is the Hellenic Republic.

Nicholas Loizou (1900-1971)

My Great Papou, Nicholas, wrote this poem
for the three great loves of his life:
his country Cyprus,
his motherland Hellenic Republic
and his five daughters:

Mahi - Battle
Eleftheria - Freedom
Elpida - Hope
Adamandia - Diamond
and
Ellada - Hellenic Republic

Foreword

For a couple of months as a far younger man I lived in a simple stone hut in a Greek olive grove with only a cistern for water. I didn't cook on the small hearth in the corner of the hut because I didn't need to. I just ate all my meals at the little taverna on the isolated bay just a 15 minute walk down the dry creek bed that ran through the grove. (Quite frankly, balancing the tripod pot over the small mound of coals in the corner of my hut was way, way beyond me—and far too scary when you are sleeping on a straw mattress!)

The days started with breakfasts of nuts, honey and yoghurt washed down with strong coffee; at simple lunches Greek salad came dolloped with the local gooey goat's cheese that had an acidic freshness which made the tomatoes sing and the chunks of cucumber became oases of sudden cool.

There, with the little local white domed church floating against the Aegean blue water, even retsina made sense—the sharp, cold wine and its smoky taste of pine pitch delicious on lips rough from a day of sea salt and sun. At night I walked home along that creek in the dark, more slowly and usually far more unsteadily, the night air thick with the smell of the same oregano that had flavoured that night's sticky goat.

I learnt that the Greek taverna was a place as much for quiet reflection as spirited discussion; a place for love or war; a place to feed the belly and the spirit. For the taverna is the kitchen table of the village or the street—a place for family and friends to gather; a watering hole, a debating hall, a gambling den and a café rolled into one.

George Calombaris's Hellenic Republic aims to capture that mood but combines it with a menu that champions the full breadth and myriad influences on peasant cuisine across the rough alliance of islands, territories and regions that we now call Greece. Hellenic Republic's menu, and the recipes contained here, are so much more than the dips and charred meats that used to characterise many aspiring earlier tavernas.

Here you'll find the fingerprints of Phoenicians, Florentines, Cypriots, Macedonians, Byzantines, Cretans and Spartans. George will especially adore that last one, given how he has bellowed the more brazen phrases from the film *300* in our quiet moments on set together filming the culinary competition TV show *MasterChef Australia*.

I have known George, and reviewed his restaurants, from his first days at Reserve, through The Press Club, and Maha, to these more egalitarian days at Hellenic. I've admired his pride in his Greek heritage and the value he puts on his extended family of aunties and cousins (which will become more and more evident as you use this book). His lollipop second serve and how few things rile him other than a few journalists. How he hates bullies. How he puts up with strange Greek grannies squeezing his cheek in the street. I subsequently realised that to Melbourne's Greek and Cypriot communities he has become a hero to rival Ang Christou from George's beloved Carlton football club. He also loves his Campari almost as much as me, has a beautiful if occasionally slightly oblique way with words which often 'basils' me, and does a very fine koala impression with nothing more than a dessert spoon.

There are flaws. My two boys reckon he's their favourite judge on *MasterChef* Australia which irks me. And he probably needs to read more so he can back up his expansive claims that the Greeks invented everything from mathematics and democracy to cookbooks, moussaka and the kilt with more than just blind faith. Everyone knows it was the Scots.

On a final point I should note that Hellenic Republic differs from my Greek Island experience in three major ways. The food's better, the décor's like a colour photograph of my fading sepia memories, and there's no Cycladean church (or powder blue Aegean) on the other side of Lygon Street. Oh, and George's Greek tavern has a roof over most of it.

This book and its recipes are a fine testament to George's love and respect for his heritage as well as his ability to look at these ideas through a lens that is thoroughly modern. As he would probably say himself: 'It's a beautiful thing'.

Matt Preston
Judge on MasterChef Australia and senior editor at
delicious. magazine and *Vogue Entertaining + Travel*

Contents

THE MENU

PROINO: BREAKFAST

PIATA: PLATES

Skara and Psitaria: Grill and Spit

Magirefta: Cooked Foods

My Mum's Greek Cypriot Heart

Glyka: Sweets

Introduction

I never understood why, when Greeks go out for dinner, the men sit together on one side and the women sit together on the other side. The men sit and solve all the problems of the world and the ladies gossip about everyone. God I love them!

I opened our taverna, Hellenic Republic, because I was sick and tired of bad taverna food. You are probably wondering why I would open a taverna after opening up The Press Club, my upmarket modern Greek restaurant. Well I have spent the last 30 years of my life eating great food at home. Yes, at home! And this has been the problem. Greeks keep all the good stuff in their homes! It's only when you enter their homes that you are not only embraced by open arms, love and humility, but also by amazing food.

So here you are. A taverna that serves home food as well. I promise you there is no molecular gastronomy here—foams, airs, liquid nitrogen, just good humble cooking.

I remember the first week we opened Hellenic Republic. I was giving the front of house team a hand to run some food to a table and placed a plate of taramosalata in front of a guest. She stopped me and asked, 'What's that?'

I announced, 'It is taramosalata'.

'I am Greek, and that is not taramosalata, it should be pink in colour.'

I laughed and excused her ignorance. I then continued to explain to her that being Greek is not a nationality or a religion; it's a state of mind. You cannot become Greek. You are born a Greek. Even though she was wrong, I was proud.

This book is not just about recipes. It's about my love for who I am and what I represent.

'Food is family, family is life, life is everything.'

Food is family,
family is life,
life is
everything.

I don't know why Greek men have worry beads. I guess it's just one of those Greek things that just happen. I have never asked my Dad why he carries them and I guess I never will.

My parents have always told me to respect all religions. There is no right or wrong. Being Greek Orthodox is more than just a religion. It's being able to believe and respect others.

Proino:Breakfast

GREEK COFFEE (NOT TURKISH!)

Ingredients
Greek coffee
Sugar (optional)
A briki (pronounced BREE-kee, see note below)
Demitasse cups
Cold water
Water glasses

Method
1. Start with very cold water. Use the demitasse cup to measure the water needed for each cup of coffee (one demitasse cup of water is about ¼ cup), and pour the water into the briki*.
2. Then add a good heaped teaspoon of coffee for each cup you are making with the appropriate sugar depending on the variations requested.
3. Place on the stove top until it boils and starts to rise. Take off before it boils over. It's the type of coffee that you must watch as it doesn't take long to boil.
4. Serve in the demitasse cup with a glass of cold water on the side.
Don't forget to serve some glyko tou koutaliou (spoon desserts) with the coffee.

Note: Greek coffee is an essential part of every pantry.
It's a great kick start to conversation or the commencement of the day and after a nap in the afternoon. This strong brew is served with kaimaki (foam) on top, but beware of draining your cup—the grounds remaining at the bottom of the cup are used for fortune telling.
*The traditional briki (small pot) is best because it allows the proper amount of foam, which adds to the unique taste. They are available from most good Middle Eastern delis.
You can enjoy Greek coffee with varying sweetness:
Sketo: no sugar, Metrio: one teaspoon of sugar, Glyko: two teaspoons of sugar.

Home-made yoghurt and berries

Serves 4

Ingredients
800ml (28fl oz) full-cream milk
1 tablespoon honey
Salt, pinch
1 cup plain Greek-style yoghurt, with live cultures
Mixed berries, to taste
Extra honey

Method
1. Bring milk to the boil, simmer for 2 minutes then leave to cool to blood temperature (38°C/100°F).
2. Whisk in honey, salt and yoghurt, then strain into sterilised glass jars, cover with cling film and leave to sit at room temperature for 12 hours, then chill till needed
3. Serve with mixed berries of your choice and drizzle with honey

Note: Also nice with toasted walnuts and honey.
To sterilise glass jars, wash and rinse jar and seals well.
Place seal, or lid if using, inside jar and fill with boiling water and leave to sit for 2 minutes.
Then place jar (not seal) upside down in oven for 10 minutes at 100°C (200°F, Gas Mark 1).
Allow to cool before using.

A food experience is not about filling the stomach, it's about warming the heart and filling the soul.

Sweet trahana porridge, manouri, strawberries and honey

Serves 4

Ingredients
1l (32fl oz) water
2 tablespoons castor sugar
500g (½lb) sweet trahana (see note below)
2 punnets strawberries
100g (3½oz) manouri cheese, crumbled (see note below)
Honey
Milk, hot or cold, to serve

Method
1. In a heavy based saucepan, bring water to the boil.
2. Add sugar and trahana and cook for 15 minutes on lowest possible setting, stirring frequently, until it resembles the consistency of porridge.
3. Divide between bowls, cover with sliced strawberries and crumbled manouri.
4. Drizzle with honey.
5. Serve with hot or cold milk.

Note: Trahana is a tiny sized pasta made of durum wheat, buttermilk and salt. It comes in two types—sweet and sour—and is a traditional Greek ingredient, also used in soups and stews.

Manouri: Literally meaning 'mothers'. It is a soft, white Greek cheese traditionally made from leftover whey after making feta.
Delicious drizzled with honey.

Hellenic Republic bircher muesli

Serves 4

Ingredients
200g (6½oz) oats
350ml (16fl oz) full-cream milk
50g (1¾oz) sultanas
200g (6½oz) yoghurt
1 punnet strawberries, pureed
2 oranges segmented, chopped
2 granny smith apples, grated, skin on
50ml (1¾ fl oz) lemon juice
25g (¾oz) almonds, flaked and toasted
25g (¾oz) sunflower seeds, toasted
Honey, to serve

Method
1. In a large bowl combine oats, milk, sultanas, yoghurt, strawberry puree, orange segments, grated apple and lemon juice.
2. Mix well and cover with cling film and refrigerate over night.
3. The next day, mix again and serve with toasted nuts and seeds and drizzle with honey.

Salad of watermelon, feta, almonds, mint and rose syrup

Serves 4

Ingredients
1 cup castor sugar
1 cup rosewater syrup (see note below)
¼ seedless watermelon
½ cup toasted flaked almonds
200g (6½oz) feta, crumbled (I use Dodoni)
¼ bunch mint

Method
1. In a saucepan, reduce castor sugar and rosewater until it starts to thicken slightly. Chill.
2. Remove skin from watermelon and cut into large chunks.
Arrange on a plate and scatter with almonds, crumbled feta and picked mint leaves.
3. Drizzle with rosewater syrup.

Note: Rosewater syrup is available in all good Middle Eastern delis.

Gigantes with baked eggs

Serves 4

Ingredients
4 cups gigantes (see gigantes recipe)
8 free-range eggs
Extra virgin olive oil
4 thick slices sourdough bread
1 head garlic, sliced in half horizontally
Sea salt, to taste

Method
1. Spoon hot gigantes into 4 dishes.
2. Crack 2 eggs into each dish, drizzle with extra virgin olive oil and sprinkle with sea salt.
3. Bake for 10 minutes in a preheated oven at 200°C (400°F, Gas Mark 6).
4. Meanwhile brush both sides of the sliced sourdough with oil.
Toast both sides under griller until golden. Rub with garlic.
5. Serve with gigantes and eggs.

MARY'S MAHI MOTHER AT 17 YEARS OLD

My Papou Michael, carpenter

Sitting around the table with my Yia Yia chatting about food and life is a religious experience. It's like a private member's club only for a selection of people. She tells me the story of when she arrived in Australia in 1955, fleeing Cyprus. She tells me that when she got off the boat, the customs officers wanted to confiscate her mortar and pestle because they thought it was a weapon. Unbelievable.

I am a very proud godfather— as the Spartans would, I would too, kill for them.

Cypriot sausage omelette, potatoes and kefalograviera

Serves 1

Ingredients
3 x 60g eggs
100ml (3½ fl oz) thickened cream
50g (1¾oz) Cypriot sausage (see note below)
1 small potato, peeled, diced and blanched until tender
2 tablespoons flat leaf parsley, shredded
50g (1¾oz) grated kefalograviera cheese
½ brown onion, sliced
Extra virgin olive oil
Salt, to taste

Method
1. Whisk together eggs and thickened cream until fluffy, and season with salt.
2. Heat non-stick pan (preferably with high edges and not too large), add 2 tablespoons extra virgin olive oil, add sausage, onion and potato and sauté for 2 minutes.
3. Add egg mix, leave on heat for 30 seconds, bringing edges into middle with spoon. Add parsley and kefalograviera and place under grill until cheese is golden.

Note: If you don't have access to any Cypriot style sausages use a good quality sausage. Kefalograviera is one of the newer Greek cheeses and is made from sheep's and goat's milk. The taste of this hard cheese is salty, with similar characteristics to pelorinder and even parmesan. Kefalograviera is sold in wheels or wedges. It has a light brown rind. It can be found at Greek or Mediterranean markets.

Toast with avocado, tomato and feta spread

Serves 4

Ingredients

200g (6½oz) feta (I use Dodoni)
100ml (3½ fl oz) milk
8 slices sourdough bread
Extra virgin olive oil
1 head garlic, sliced in half horizontally
4 vine ripened tomatoes
2 ripe avocados
2 tablespoons fresh picked oregano
Sea salt, to taste

Method

1. Blend feta with milk until smooth.
2. Brush sourdough with extra virgin olive oil and grill on both sides.
3. Rub garlic halves over bread.
Spread feta evenly over slices of bread
4. Top each slice of toast with mashed avocado and sliced tomato.
Sprinkle with a pinch of fresh oregano, sea salt and extra virgin olive oil.

Smoked lamb ham sandwich

Serves 4

Ingredients
2 tablespoons extra virgin olive oil
4 free-range eggs
8 slices sourdough bread
Extra virgin olive oil
1 head garlic, sliced in half horizontally
50g (1¾oz) kefalograviera cheese
150g (5oz) shaved smoked lamb ham

Method
1. In a non-stick pan, heat olive oil and gently fry eggs to liking.
2. Brush sourdough with olive oil, grill on both sides, then rub with garlic halves.
3. Shave kefalograviera with peeler.
4. To assemble, place smoked lamb ham on toast, top with fried egg and kefalograviera cheese.

Note: Our butcher Carlo, from Chef's Choice, cures and smokes boned legs of lamb, however you can replace the smoked lamb ham with finely shaved ham of your choice.

Information

per package: 227

1,1g

per 100gr

0Kj

0g

0g

0g

0g

0g

0g

0g

39,3g

3,7mg

KALAS

Golden

Ouzo-cured salmon, scrambled eggs

Serves 4

Ingredients
200g (6½oz) table salt
100g (3½oz) sugar
5 pieces star anise, roughly smashed
100ml (3½ oz) ouzo (Plomari)
200g (6½oz) boneless salmon fillet, skin on
8 free-range eggs
300ml (10fl oz) thickened cream
Salt, to taste
4 slices sourdough bread
1 tablespoon extra virgin olive oil
1 head garlic, sliced in half horizontally
1 tablespoon unsalted butter
2 tablespoons flat leaf parsley, shredded

Method
1. In a bowl, mix sugar, salt, star anise and ouzo.
2. In a suitable container or plate, place salmon skin-side down, cover with curing mix, cling film and refrigerate for 12 hours.
3. Remove from fridge, wash mix from salmon and pat dry. Slice salmon on an angle without cutting through the skin.
4. Whisk eggs with thickened cream until light and fluffy, season with salt.
5. Brush sourdough with extra virgin olive oil and grill on both sides. Rub garlic on toast.
6. Lay smoked salmon over sourdough and place on a plate ready for the eggs.
7. Place a non-stick frying pan over medium to high heat for 2 minutes. Add extra virgin olive oil, butter and quickly add egg mix and parsley just before butter starts to colour.
8. Quickly stir with wooden spoon, remove from heat whilst they are still slightly under cooked so that they finish cooking with residual heat from pan.
9. Spoon over the salmon and serve.

Roasted beetroot and feta muffins

Makes 9

Ingredients
1 cup self-raising flour
1 cup wholemeal flour
½ teaspoon salt
2 tablespoons baking powder
125ml (4¼fl oz) extra virgin olive oil
1 cup full-cream milk
1 egg
2 whole beetroot, roasted, peeled and diced into 1cm cubes (see note below)
200g (6½oz) feta (I use Dodoni)

Method
1. Pre-heat oven to 190°C (375°F, Gas Mark 5).
Sift flours, salt and baking powder into bowl.
2. Whisk olive oil, milk and egg together, then with a wooden spoon
stir into dry ingredients until just combined.
3. Fold in diced beetroot and crumbled feta.
4. Spoon mixture into greased muffin trays lined with muffin patties
and bake in a pre-heated oven for 15 minutes
(or until a skewer inserted comes out clean).

Note: To roast beetroot, lay foil on bench, place beetroot on top and drizzle with
extra virgin olive oil, salt, cloves and garlic.
Wrap with foil and bake at 180°C (350°F, Gas Mark 4) for approximately 1 hour until
skewer inserts easily. Skin should remove easily while beets are still warm.

Spanakopita, poached eggs

Serves 4

Ingredients
1 brown onion, sliced
1 garlic clove, sliced
500g (17½oz) spinach
100g (3½oz) ricotta, crumbled
100g (3½oz) feta (I use Dodoni), crumbled
1 packet filo pastry
200ml (7fl oz) extra virgin olive oil
¼ cup white vinegar
4 fresh free-range eggs
Salt, to taste

Method
1. Pre-heat oven. Sauté sliced onion with garlic until tender.
2. Add spinach and half wilt, remove from heat, allow to cool. Squeeze out excess moisture. This is very important, otherwise it will make the pastry soggy.
3. Add ricotta and feta and combine evenly. Season to taste with salt.
4. Lay a sheet of pastry on bench, brushing liberally with olive oil. Repeat until it is 5 layers deep.
5. Place mixture in a line on one edge and roll up. Coil up to look like a snail, tucking ends under.
6. Bake at 180°C (350°F, Gas Mark 4, Gas Mark 4) for 14 minutes or until golden brown.
7. Bring a large saucepan of water to the boil, add vinegar and adjust heat until just simmering. Crack eggs into water. If they are fresh they will stay together nicely. Be careful not to overcrowd—you may need to cook in two batches.
8. Simmer gently for 2½ minutes or to liking and remove with slotted spoon. Season with salt. Place on top of spanakopita so that when eating yolk runs over spanakopita. Drizzle with olive oil and serve.

Note: We are lucky enough to have a supplier who makes beautiful homemade filo pastry which is more flexible and less likely to crack when rolling. If you are having trouble rolling the filo make a large rectangle spanakopita instead and cut into portions.

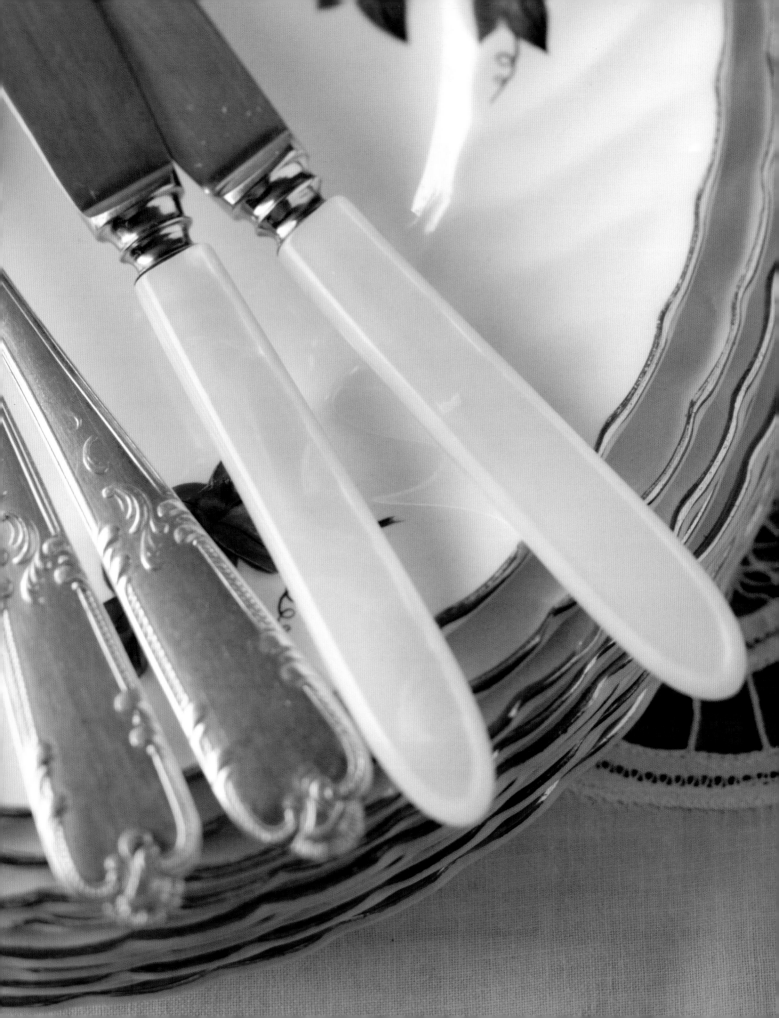

Piata:Plates

Horiatiki salata
Village salad

Serves 4

Ingredients
8 ripe tomatoes, coarsely cut
1 continental cucumber, peeled, deseeded and rustic cut
¼ small red onion, thinly sliced
½ green capsicum, thinly sliced
200g (6½oz) marinated kalamata olives
50g (1¾oz) feta (I use Dodoni), sliced thick
1 pinch dried oregano
1 pinch salt
Olive oil, to taste
Red wine vinegar, to taste

Method
1. Toss tomatoes, cucumber, onion, capsicum, olives and olive oil together.
2. Arrange in a salad bowl and top with crumbled feta, sprinkle with oregano and add a pinch of salt.
3. Dress liberally with olive oil and red wine vinegar.

Olives

Serves 4

Ingredients
1 tablespoon lemon thyme, finely chopped
2 cloves garlic, peeled and finely sliced
Zest of 1 orange (use peeler for longer strips)
100ml (3½ fl oz) extra virgin olive oil
100g (3½oz) kalamata olives
100g (3½oz) throumbes olives
100g (3½oz) blonde chalkidikis olives

Method
1. Pre-heat oven. Combine lemon thyme, garlic, orange zest and olive oil in a pot and bring
to the boil then set aside to infuse.
2. Drain any juices from olives if any, by soaking them in hot water for 1 hour.
Drain and repeat.
3. Drain olives and add to a deep tray or baking dish. Cover with infused oil
and place in an oven at 120°C (250°F, Gas Mark 1) for 1 hour.
4. Remove olives, drain and serve warm.

Note: To keep olives, store in a sterilised jar with the marinade.
Keep infused oils for salad dressing.

Kalamata

A medium size, almond shaped Greek olive that ranges from black to purple in colour, with a soft meat. It is a brine-cured, stone cracked olive that is slit, packed in vinegar, and cured to produce a rich, somewhat sour to fruity flavour.

Throumbes

A dried olive that is naturally shrivelled on the branch. Throumbes olives are the only olive which can be eaten directly from the tree.

Chalkidikis

A large, pale green coloured Greek olive that is oval in shape and usually harvested when it is young. It is brine-cured and has a firm textured meat providing a soft, full flavour, which is slightly tart and somewhat peppery. This olive is grown in the Halkidiki region of Greece, adjacent to Mount Athos. This is why it is also referred to as a Mount Athos or Halkidiki olive, as Halkidiki and Chalkidiki are used interchangeably as a name for the Central Macedonian region of Greece where these olives are grown.

Melizanosalata
Eggplant (aubergine) dip, red wine onions

Serves 4

Ingredients
3 whole eggplants (aubergine)
50ml (1¾ fl oz) red wine vinegar
2 teaspoons tahini
2 teaspoons roasted garlic puree
1 red onion, sliced
300ml (10fl oz) red wine
1 tablespoon sugar
Salt, to taste
150ml (5fl oz) extra virgin olive oil

Method
1. Using a fork, prick eggplant and place on a hot char-grill until tender.
2. Once cool enough to handle, halve lengthways and scoop out flesh.
3. Hang flesh in a sieve overnight to remove excess liquid.
4. Place flesh in a food processor and blend to create a smooth puree.
5. Add red wine vinegar, tahini, garlic and season with salt while constantly blitzing.
As you drizzle in olive oil, the mixture will begin to whiten.
6. Reduce red wine and sugar in a pan until a syrup consistency.
7. Add red onion, stir and cover with lid and steam for 5 minutes to soften onions.
Remove lid and stir until liquid is almost evaporated. Season with salt.
8. Place the melizanosalata into small bowls
and serve with the red onion.

Patzari
Cumin roasted beetroot, yoghurt

Serves 4

Ingredients
600g (21oz) beetroot
1 tablespoon chopped thyme
½ head garlic, skin on, roughly chopped
40ml (1⅓ fl oz) vegetable oil
2 teaspoons cumin seeds, toasted and crushed
40ml (1⅓ fl oz) extra virgin olive oil
20ml (⅔ fl oz) sherry vinegar
1 tablespoon yoghurt
1 tablespoon coriander, shredded
Salt, to taste

Method
1. Pre-heat oven. Place whole beetroots in a roasting tray and scatter with thyme and garlic. Drizzle with vegetable oil, cover with foil and bake at 180°C (350°F, Gas Mark 4) for 1 hour or until a skewer passes though easily.
2. Once cool, using gloves, peel beetroots and cut into rough dice.
3. Combine cumin seeds, olive oil and sherry vinegar and pour over cut beetroots.
4. Mix yoghurt and coriander through beetroot, season with salt and serve.

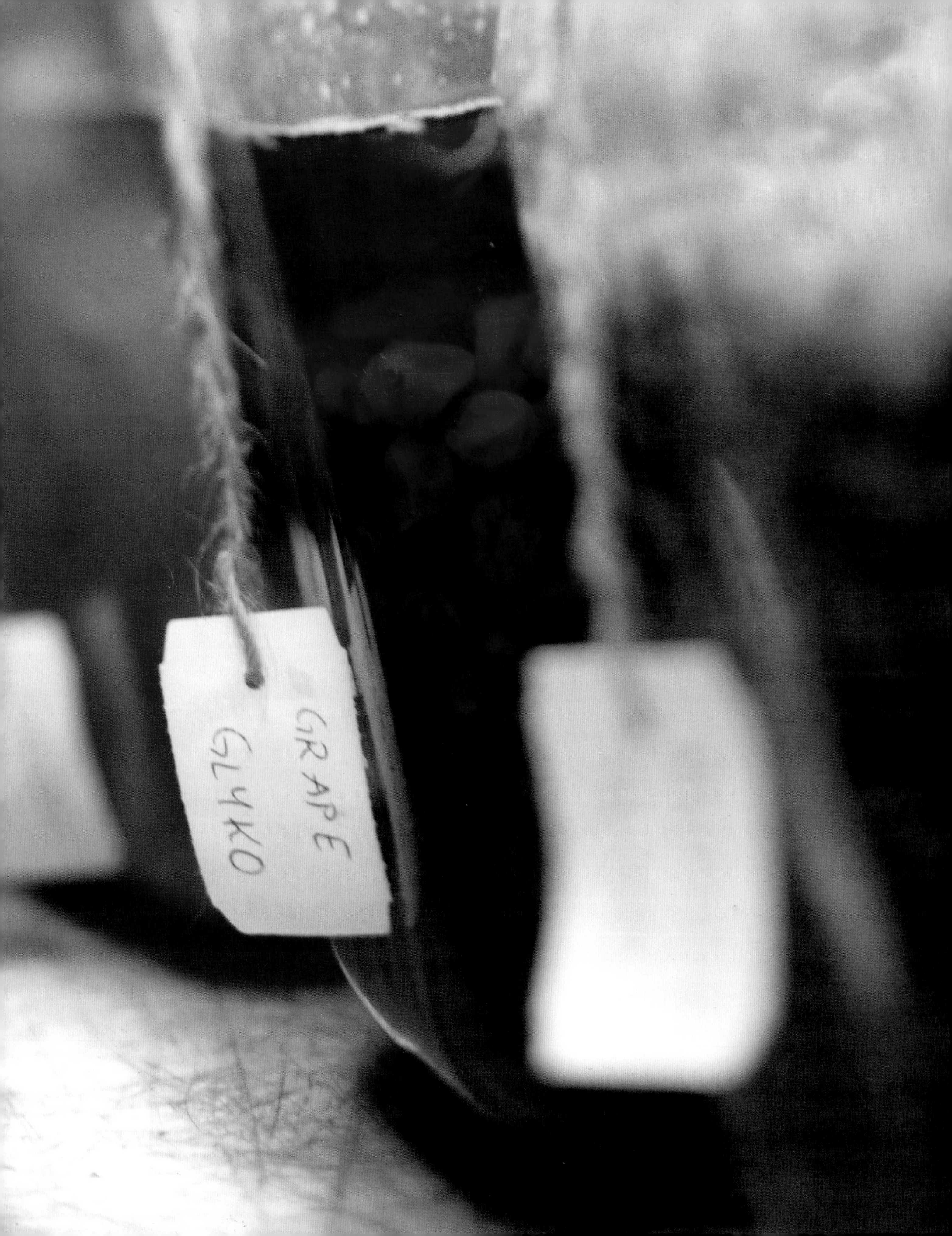
GRAPE
GLYKO

I always pay homage to the chef that creates a recipe. For me, the peppered figs are an inspiration from my mate David from Perama Restaurant in Sydney. Thanks, Agapi.

Peppered figs

Serves 4

Ingredients
100g (3½oz) dried baby figs
1 tablespoon Attiki honey
2 teaspoons balsamic vinegar
1 tablespoon black pepper, cracked
1 cinnamon quill
1 small bay leaf
3 cloves
Water to cover

Method
1. Place figs, honey, balsamic vinegar, black pepper, cinnamon quill, bay leaf and cloves in a saucepan. Add water and bring to the boil.
2. Reduce to a simmer, cover and cook gently until tender. Preserve in a sterilised jar.

Note: Serve on top of grilled haloumi. It's delicious!

It's like a ritual, I am sure it's in the Orthodox bible. When it comes to dinner time we all sit around the table together as a family. Never do we start eating until mum sits down and never do we get up until dad is finished. There is always wine on the table, and if kids want to try some, they can. I guess that's why we are not binge drinkers in our adult life—alcohol was not foreign to us.

At the dinner table, there is always a horiatiki of some description, doused with olive oil and vinegar. Dad always waits for us to finish the salad, then brings it close to his chin and proceeds to dip the bread in, soaking up all the salad oils, vinegars, juice from home-grown tomatoes, oregano and salty feta. I loved this at a young age. I would watch my father and feel inspired.

My mother would do without the shirt on her back to feed us kids great food. She would not only feed us, she would love us!

Toursi
Pickled vegetables

Serves 4

Ingredients
100ml (3½ fl oz) Attiki honey
200ml (7fl oz) extra virgin olive oil
600ml (20fl oz) white wine vinegar
100g (3½oz) cauliflower, cut into florets
100g (3½oz) cabbage, cut thumb size
100g (3½oz) medium carrots, angle sliced
100g (3½oz) zucchini, angle sliced, raw
100g (3½oz) leek, thinly sliced, raw
25g (¾oz) celery, thinly sliced, raw
2 tablespoons chopped coriander
Extra virgin olive oil
Salt, to taste

Method
1. Mix honey, extra virgin olive oil and vinegar until well combined.
2. Steam cauliflower, cabbage and carrots separately until just cooked.
3. Combine steamed cauliflower, cabbage, carrot, raw zucchini, raw leek and raw celery.
Pour pickling mixture over vegetables.
4. Seal into a sterilised jar and leave for two days.
5. To serve, drain pickled vegetables and toss with coriander,
olive oil and season with salt.

Taramosalata
Real white fish roe dip

Serves 4

Ingredients
4 slices white bread, crusts removed
300ml (10fl oz) water to cover
40g (1½oz) brown onion, roughly chopped
100g (3½oz) salted white cod roe paste
50ml (2fl oz) lemon juice
550ml (19fl oz) olive oil

Method
1. Cover bread with water and soak overnight.
2. Blend onion in a food processor/blender until smooth.
Drop in fish roe and continue to blend.
3. Squeeze moisture from bread and add to food processor, blending.
Add lemon juice and continue to blend until mixture is completely smooth.
4. Slowly drizzle in olive oil to create an emulsion, as you would for a mayonnaise.
5. If too thick, loosen with a little hot water.
6. Serve with grilled pita bread

Note: Many people, including Greeks, think taramosalata is pink, but it is
traditionally made with roe, not caviar.

There is no better
feeling than seeing the
joy on people's faces as
they eat your food.
I am so lucky, I
thank God every day
for my health, family
and my love for food.

Tzatziki
Cucumber, dill, garlic, olive oil and yoghurt dip

Serves 4

Ingredients
1 cucumber, peeled, deseeded, grated
400g (13oz) thick Greek-style yoghurt
3 cloves garlic, roasted and pureed
30ml (1fl oz) white vinegar
40ml (1½fl oz) extra virgin olive oil
1 tablespoon dill, shredded
Salt, to taste

Method
1. Sprinkle cucumber with ½ teaspoon salt.
2. Leave grated cucumber overnight in colander to extract excess juices.
3. Place yoghurt, garlic, vinegar, extra virgin olive oil and dill into a large bowl.
Season with salt to taste.
4. Squeeze excess liquid from cucumber and add to yoghurt.
5. Mix well and season to taste.
6. Serve with grilled pita bread.

I look at my Papou George in this picture and it reminds me of what life is all about. If you can first love yourself, then you can love others. I never met him but anyone that did says I am very like him. I guess this picture explains it. He enjoyed making people happy through his music. I like to make people happy through my food.

Pipperies florinis
Marinated peppers in olive oil and vinegar

Serves 4

Ingredients
40ml (1½fl oz) sherry vinegar
20ml (2/3fl oz) extra virgin olive oil
1 stalk rosemary, bruised
1 clove garlic, finely shaved
12 long green capsicums (peppers), char-grilled and peeled
Salt, to taste

Method
1. Combine sherry vinegar, olive oil, garlic and rosemary.
2. Pour vinaigrette over grilled capsicum.
3. Season well with salt.
4. Serve at room temperature.

Note: To grill capsicums, season wih salt and brush with olive oil and char-grill until they blister. Place in a bowl and cling film so they sweat. Once cool, peel skin off and put aside to be marinated. To bruise rosemary, tap lightly with the back of a knife.

TIGANITES PATATES
HAND-CUT POTATOES COOKED
IN OLIVE OIL, OREGANO

Serves 4

Ingredients
10 potatoes, suitable for frying
Olive oil (to fill fryer)
Salt, to taste
Dried mountain oregano, to season

Method
1. Wash potatoes well to remove any soil from surface.
Cut into chips the thickness of your finger.
2. Steam potatoes for approximately 10 minutes or until just tender.
Place in fridge to dry surface of potato.
3. Blanch potatoes at 130°C (250°F, Gas Mark 1) in deep fryer filled with olive oil.
Place on clean tea towel in fridge to dry out.
4. Turn up the heat to 180°C (350°F, Gas Mark 4) and refry potatoes until crispy.
Serve sprinkled with salt and oregano.

Note: It's important to use a potato that is suitable for frying as different varieties may cause chips to become dark and soggy. If in doubt, ask you local grocer.

The great thing about the Hellenic table is the generosity of spirit. Never stop sharing never stop giving and never stop eating and drinking.

Kοτοpουλο Ανγολεμονο
Chicken, egg and lemon soup

Serves 4

Ingredients
1 whole small chicken, organic
Water, to cover
½ cup arborio rice
2 eggs
Lemon juice, to taste
Salt, to taste

Method
1. Wash the inside of the chicken under a tap.
2. Place chicken in a large pot, cover with water and simmer gently for 1½ hours.
3. Remove chicken from stock and once cool, remove skin and flesh. Shred flesh.
Pass stock through fine sieve. Bring stock to the boil and reduce until flavour is intense.
4. Boil rice until tender, strain and allow to cool on a tray.
5. To serve, place some chicken and rice into the base of a bowl.
6. Break eggs into a large saucepan. Whisk while pouring in hot stock.
Pour over chicken and rice in bowls.
7. Season with lemon juice and salt.

Note: Delicious when you are ill!
This picture shows the shredded chicken before the stock is added.

Gigantes
Giant beans with tomato and olive oil

Serves 4

Ingredients
250g (1¾oz) gigantes beans, soaked overnight
¼ cup extra virgin olive oil
½ brown onion, finely diced
1 garlic clove, finely sliced
½ cup carrots, finely chopped
½ cup celery, finely chopped
½ tablespoon dried oregano
½ tablespoon thyme, finely chopped
½ tablespoon tomato paste
75ml (2½fl oz) sherry vinegar
500g (3oz) chopped tomato
250ml (1¾fl oz) water
Salt, to taste
¼ bunch flat leaf parsley, roughly chopped

Method
1. Drain soaked beans and place in a large pot, cover well with water
and bring to the boil.
2. Reduce to a simmer and cook until tender. Strain and keep aside.
3. Heat oil in a pot and cook onion for 3 minutes.
4. Add garlic, carrots, celery, oregano, thyme and tomato paste. Stir over a low heat
for 3 minutes. Deglaze with sherry vinegar.
5. Add tomatoes and water and bring to the boil. Stir in beans.
6. Cover with foil and bake for 1 hour at 180°C (350°F, Gas Mark 4)
7. Season well with salt. Finish with parsley and extra olive oil.

Notes: Gigantes are traditional Greek butter beans that come from Kastoria.
They can be black or white in colour.

GEMISTA
VEGETABLES STUFFED WITH HERB RICE

Serves 4

Ingredients
4 red capsicums (peppers), top cut off (to form a lid), seeds scooped out
4 zucchini (courgettes), tops cut off (to form a lid), flesh scooped out
4 medium vine ripened tomatoes, top cut off to form a lid
2 tablespoons castor sugar
1 tablespoon olive oil
1 small brown onion, finely diced
1 garlic clove, finely diced
1 cup long grain rice
1 teaspoon mint, shredded
2 tablespoons flat leaf parsley, shredded
1 pinch black pepper
2 large potatoes
Salt, to taste

Method
1. Scoop out the tomato pulp, being careful not to break the skin. Blend the pulp with the castor sugar and set aside.
2. Heat the olive oil in a saucepan and sauté onion and garlic until soft.
Add the rice and cook for a few minutes.
3. Add enough of tomato mixture to cover rice and cook for a few minutes.
Remove from the heat, add mint and parsley.
Add pepper and season with salt.
4. Fill vegetables with mixture being careful not to overstuff.
Place vegetables side by side in a baking tray. In between vegetables use cut potato wedges to fill in the gaps and support the stuffed vegetables.
5. Add enough water until it is half covering the vegetables. Cover with foil.
6. Bake at 160°C (325°F, Gas Mark 4) for 40 minutes until rice is cooked.

I hate the word celebrity chef. Let's get this one straight; I was a cook before I became a chef and I am a chef that is on TV. That makes me a chef, that's who I am.

Dolmathakia
Stuffed vine leaves with yoghurt

Serves 4

Ingredients
30 vine leaves
Water, to soak
300g (10½oz) brown onions, finely diced
3 tablespoons blended oil
100g (3½oz) long grain rice, washed
1 pinch allspice
1 pinch ground cinnamon
Salt, to taste
150ml (1¾fl oz) water
¼ bunch flat leaf parsley, shredded
¼ bunch dill, shredded
250ml (1¾fl oz) extra virgin olive oil
250g (8¾oz) yoghurt

Method
1. Soak vine leaves in water to remove saltiness.
Separate leaves and set aside unusable ones.
2. Sauté onions in oil until tender. Add rice and cook for a few minutes.
3. Add allspice and cinnamon. Season with salt.
4. Pour in water, cover and cook in oven at 180°C (350°F, Gas Mark 4) until all liquid
has evaporated. Stir through parsley and dill.
5. Roll dolmathakia.

6. Line a steamer with broken or small (unusable) vine leaves. Place rolled dolmathakia on these, lining from the outside in. Place a plate on top of the dolmathakia to hold them down and allow them to keep their shape.

7. Place inside a pot of boiling water, cover with a lid and allow to steam for 45 minutes. Lift plate off and pour olive oil over dolmathakia.

8. Replace plate and leave untouched in fridge for minimum 6 hours.

9. Serve with yoghurt and olive oil.

Notes:

To roll dolmathakia: Place vine leaf rough side up, remove stem.

Place 2 teaspoons of mixture on bottom part of leaf and bring up leaf to cover mixture.

Bring in sides firmly but not too tightly and roll. Place seam-side down inside steamer.

Allow dolmathakia to cool in refrigerator with plate on top to prevent the leaf turning black.

I hate clichés about Greek food. Most people think Greek cuisine is about bad dips and fried food. Let me tell you, it's about healthy eating. Fresh, simple and elegant. But above all, soulful.

Dakos
Cretan barley rusk

Serves 4

Ingredients

4 small ripe tomatoes
4 barley rusks (dakos)
1 tablespoon dried oregano
1 teaspoon salt
20 baby capsicums (peppers), roasted until soft
50ml (1¾ fl oz) sherry vinegar
50ml (1¾ fl oz) olive oil
2 sprigs thyme, washed
50g (1¾oz) red onions, finely diced
50g (1¾oz) kalamata olives
50g (1¾oz) feta (I use Dodoni), crumbled
1 tablespoon baby capers
4 sprigs purslane, picked and washed (Mediterranean leaf)
30ml (1fl oz) olive oil

Method

1. Grate tomato and spread over barley rusk. Sprinkle liberally with oregano, olive oil and salt. Leave overnight to soften.
2. Marinate roasted capsicums with sherry vinegar, olive oil and thyme.
3. Combine red onion, capsicum, olives, feta, capers and purslane and drizzle with olive oil.
4. Place salad over dakos and eat!

Note: Purslane can be replaced with flat leaf parsley.
Dakos are a barley rusk cripsbread available from most Middle Eastern delis.

Cypriot burghul
wheat salad

Serves 4

Ingredients
100g (1¾oz) cracked burghul wheat
3 bunches coriander, including half stems, shredded
5 Roma tomatoes, finely diced, deseeded
½ red onion, finely diced
½ lemon, zested
1 lemon, juiced
½ cup olive oil
Salt, to taste

Method
1. Soak burghul wheat in hot tap water for 10 minutes.
Pour into strainer and leave for 2 hours.
2. Place coriander, tomatoes, onion, lemon zest, lemon juice
and olive oil to burghul in a bowl.
3. Season well with salt and eat straight away.

Fig and olive relish

Ingredients
300g (10½oz) dried figs
150g (1¾oz) pitted kalamata olives
100g (3½oz) red wine vinegar
100g (3½oz) brown sugar

Method
1. Soak figs overnight in 1 litre of water.
2. Drain water and save 100mls of this liquid.
Add all ingredients to the pot and simmer gently for 20 minutes.
3. Remove from heat, cool for 5 minutes then pulse in blender
until smooth texture is achieved.
4. Chill and serve with cheese.

Fava
yellow split pea dip

Serves 8

Ingredients
1¾ cups yellow split peas
1 carrot, peeled and sliced
1 brown onion, peeled and cut into quarters
1 stick celery, sliced
2 cloves garlic, peeled
3 tablespoons extra virgin olive oil
1 tablespoon salt

Shallot dressing
2 shallots (scallion), finely diced
1 tablespoon thyme, finely chopped
3 tablespoons red wine vinegar
3 tablespoons extra virgin olive oil

Method
1. Soak split peas overnight in 1000ml (1 litre) water.
2. Strain split peas, cover in a pot with 1 litre water and bring to the boil then strain.
3. Add split peas back to the pot with carrot, onion, celery, garlic
and 1000ml (1 litre) water.
4. Bring to the boil; remove any scum that comes to the surface and simmer until split peas
are tender, approximately 45 minutes.
5. While still hot, blend with a stick blender; add extra virgin olive oil and season with salt. if
too thick add a little hot water to loosen.
6. To make shallot dressing, mix together shallots, thyme,
red wine vinegar and extra virgin olive oil.
7. Serve fava at room temperature with shallot dressing over top.

BRIAM
BAKED CRETAN VEGETABLES

Serves 4

Ingredients

1 green capsicum (pepper) cut into 2cm (1in) cubes
1 large eggplant (aubergine) cut into 2cm (1in) cubes
2 medium zucchini (courgette) sliced on an angle 1cm (½in) thick
5 tomatoes, grated
2 red onions, sliced 1cm (½in) rings
3 cloves garlic, crushed
1 teaspoon cumin powder
1 teaspoon dried oregano
250ml (1¾fl oz) water
125ml (4¼fl oz) extra virgin olive oil
1 bunch flat leaf parsley, shredded
½ cup thick yoghurt, plus extra to serve
Small pinch saffron threads
2 tablespoons milk

Method

1. Mix eggplant, zucchini, tomatoes, capsicum, onion, garlic, cumin, oregano, water and
olive oil until well coated in olive oil and season with salt.
2. Spread out on oven tray and bake in a pre-heated oven at
200°C (400°F, Gas Mark 6) for 40 minutes until soft.
Gently shake tray every 10 minutes to avoid sticking.
Avoid mixing with spoon, you don't want to mash the vegetables.
3. Leave vegetables to cool to room temperature.
Check seasoning, finish with parsley leave at room temperature.
4. Warm milk and saffron threads, leave to cool to room temperature.
Pass through a fine sieve pressing milk from remaining threads.
5. Mix with yoghurt and serve with briam.

Skara and Psitaria: Grill and Spit

Sheftalies
Cypriot patties

Serves 4

Ingredients
1 large brown onion, finely diced
200g (6½oz) lamb mince
200g (6½oz) pork mince
½ bunch parsley, shredded
Freshly cracked black pepper, to taste
1 tablespoon mint, finely chopped
1 cup fresh breadcrumbs
1 pinch ground cinnamon
100g caul fat (soaked overnight in salty water)
Salt to taste

Method
1. Sauté onion until tender and allow to cool fully. Add lamb mince, pork mince, parsley, black pepper, mint, breadcrumbs, cinnamon and knead until well combined.
2. Drain water from caul fat, rinse with fresh water until the water runs clear.
3. Roll mince into 5cm (2in) ovals, flatten slightly and wrap in caul fat and refrigerate to firm up.
4. Chargrill over a gentle heat until cooked through, serve with fresh lemon.

Note: Caul fat is the fatty membrane which surrounds the internal organs of some animals. It is often used as a natural sausage casing. Speak to your local butcher.

LATHOLEMONO
Olive oil and lemon dressing

Serves 4

Ingredients
100ml (3½ fl oz) lemon juice
1 teaspoon Dijon mustard
100ml (3½ fl oz) extra virgin olive oil
1 teaspoon dried oregano
Salt to taste

Method
1. Place lemon juice and Dijon mustard in a food processor and blend well.
2. Slowly drizzle in olive oil, blitzing constantly to create an emulsion.
3. Season well with salt.
4. Add enough oregano to flavour.

Note: All ingredients <u>must</u> be at room temperature otherwise mix will split.
This is a great dressing for fish, chicken and lamb.

Chargrilled octopus

Serves 4

Ingredients
1 bunch of lemon thyme washed, finely chopped
4 cloves garlic, finely sliced
3 shallots (scallions), finely diced
½ bunch rosemary, chopped
500ml (16fl oz) red wine vinegar
500ml (16fl oz) olive oil
1kg (2.2lb) octopus, beaten
5 litres water
500ml (16fl oz) white vinegar
Salt, to taste

Method
1. In a large bowl mix thyme, garlic, shallots, rosemary, red wine vinegar
and olive oil, mix well.
2. Peel outside membrane off the octopus without removing suckers.
Cut into separate legs.
3. Bring 5 litres of water and the white vinegar to the boil then add octopus to the pot.
Simmer without boiling for 10 minutes, remove and add to marinade whilst hot.
4. Mix octopus into marinade with hands, cover and refrigerate for at least 2 hours.
5. Remove excess marinade from octopus and cook for
2 minutes each side on a hot grill.
Cut into large pieces. Season to taste.

Lamb souvlaki

Serves 4

Ingredients

100ml (3½ fl oz) extra virgin olive oil
500g (17½oz) lamb shoulder, boned
5 cloves garlic, halved vertically
1 sprig rosemary
1 sprig lemon thyme
125ml (4¼fl oz) white wine
Salt, to taste
Black pepper, to taste
400ml (13½fl oz) chicken stock
4 pita breads
Extra virgin olive oil, to brush
4 sheets grease-proof paper
50g (1¾oz) Dijon mustard
25g (¾oz) patates tiganites (see tiganites recipe page 92)
¼ red onion, finely sliced
¼ bunch flat leaf parsley, leaves picked

Method

1. Heat olive oil in a heavy based pot and seal lamb.
Add garlic, rosemary, thyme and white wine.
Reduce liquid by two-thirds and season with salt and black pepper.
2. Add chicken stock and braise until tender for 2½ hours at 165°C (320°F).
3. Remove meat, strain liquid into a clean pot. Bring to the boil, remove scum and reduce to a sauce consistency.
4. Shred lamb and add to sauce. Keep warm.
5. Brush pita breads with olive oil and warm in a hot oven for 3 minutes.
6. Lay out grease proof paper. Place a pita on top, smear with Dijon mustard.
Top with lamb, patates tiganites, onion and parsley.
7. Roll up and eat!

THE GREEK FETA
DODO

Barbequed Feta with Asparagus

Preparation Time: 5 Minutes   Cooking Time: 5 Minutes

Serves: 4

1 bunch asparagus

Sea salt and cracked pepper

My mama is a great storyteller and she told me this story. Once upon a time in 1941 a young girl went to visit her grandfather. He had survived the 'population exchange' of 1922 from Asia Minor and moved to Greece, his other homeland, with his surviving five siblings. The other 13 had died from the ravages of war.

His wife had escaped with the two youngest in "freedom boats" sent by the Greeks. His wealth had been lost. Yianni Hatzikostaki had been a mayor of Rias Dere and merchant of Damascus, and was a prominent citizen who traded in Ismir. In Greece his last occupation was as a garlic and lemon street seller, known to everyone as the "Asia Minor gentleman with the kind eyes." He never took anything for granted and always had a humbling demeanour.

The last time his granddaughter came to see him in the shell-shocked house in Kaisariani, she was eight. She noticed him sitting still in the house and as she approached him closer, an ant crawled out of his mouth. He was dead.

My great grandfather died before he saw the end of World War II and the German occupation, civil war, post-civil war turmoil and junta period. His granddaughter would also endure a hard life, his legacy of pride and humility carrying on.

I grew up in a Greek Australian household. I knew that we were different. I didn't know what an Anzac biscuit was and I didn't understand people who didn't move their hands while they spoke.

Llike many Greeks, my parents settled in Prahran in Melbourne because it was close to the market and the city.

Mama is Athenian and while as she didn't speak English, she was a city slicker.

My parents filled me with pride and humility from a young age, retelling the stories of my ancestors and their plights. It seemed like all the generations before me were either immigrants or refugees. Our family were constantly moving to and from Greece. That is our nature—from Homer's Odyssey to modern day Anesti Giannakodakis, my father.

What is it to be us? It's a sense of adventure, duty, pride, humility and the determination to survive and let the people transcend all time. And of course the love of living. Never take any day for granted. Many were lost on their journey from hardship but I see Greeks all around me now wherever I walk and work.

Our people understand this philosophy even if they were not born in Greece or haven't had anything to do with Greeks. It's a state of mind, a way of living, a thirst to excel in humanity and communicate with and love one another.

To be truly Hellene one must have seeking eyes and an open heart. The more you embrace the more unique life can be. I guess that's why I am in hospitality and if ever I was taught humility it was from my parents. I was born to serve and what is 'to serve' but to give a little happiness.

Angie Giannakodakis

Marinade for pork

Makes 750ml (3 cups, 24fl oz)

Ingredients
500ml (16fl oz) olive oil
250ml (8fl oz) orange juice
3 cloves garlic, crushed
3 tablespoons Dijon mustard
2 tablespoons soy sauce
1 tablespoon fresh thyme, chopped
1 teaspoon toasted fennel seeds, crushed

Method
Combine ingredients and marinate pork 12 hours before cooking.

Notes: Great on cuts such as belly and shoulder, even suckling pigs if you're putting on the rotisserie. Add 2 tablespoons of water to marinade to use this as a baste.

Marinade for seafood

Makes 250ml (1 cup, 8fl oz)

Ingredients
350ml (12½fl oz) olive oil
Juice and zest from 1 lemon
2 cloves garlic, crushed
1 tablespoon honey
1 tablespoon parsley, chopped
1 tablespoon dill, chopped
1 tablespoon fresh thyme, chopped
2 shallots (scallions), finely diced

Method
Combine all ingredients and cover seafood.
Refrigerate and leave for at least 2 hours.

Notes: Great for all seafood. We use this on our prawns (shrimp) and whole fish
but you can also use it on chicken.

Travis is not only at the helm at Hellenic Republic, he is my mate. He is also an amazing chef and is the backbone to food there. If other chefs were half of Travis, they would also be great.

Marinade for poultry

Makes 350ml (1 cup, 8fl oz)

Ingredients
100ml (3½fl oz) white wine
250ml (8fl oz) olive oil
Juice and zest of 2 lemons
2 cloves garlic, crushed
2 tablespoons brown sugar
1 tablespoon dried oregano
1 tablespoon fresh rosemary, chopped
1 tablespoon fresh thyme, chopped
1 teaspoon toasted cumin seeds, crushed
1 teaspoon toasted coriander seeds, crushed

Method
Combine ingredients, marinate meat for a minimum of 12 hours.

Note: This is a great marinade for chicken and can also be used on fish. It can also be used as a baste for spit-roasted meats.

Marinade for lamb and beef

Makes 700ml (3 cups, 24fl oz)

Ingredients
450ml (14¼fl oz) olive oil
250ml (8fl oz) orange juice
3 cloves garlic, crushed
2 tablespoons Dijon mustard
4 tablespoons honey
2 tablespoons olive oil
1 tablespoon fresh thyme, chopped
1 brown onion, grated

Method
Combine ingredients and marinate meat for a minimum of 12 hours.

Note: This is a great marinade for lamb and beef. Marinade can also be used for meats on the spit or, if using on grill, remove excess marinade before cooking.

Magirefta:
Cooked Foods

Pork fricassee
Slow-cooked in celery, lettuce and dill

Serves 4

Ingredients
1kg (2.2lb) pork shoulder, diced
100ml (3½fl oz) extra virgin olive oil
1 brown onion, sliced
2 celery stalks, sliced
2 sticks spring onions, sliced—keep white and green separate
Salt, to taste
Black pepper, to taste
Water, to just cover
1 head of iceberg lettuce, roughly chopped
2 tablespoons dill, shredded
2 tablespoons parsley, shredded
3 eggs
200ml (7fl oz) lemon juice
40g (1½ oz) butter, diced

Method
1. Fry and seal pork in extra virgin olive oil until browned.
2. Add onion, celery and whites of spring onion and cook until tender. Season with salt and cracked pepper, cover with water and braise
for 3 hours at 170°C (325°F, Gas Mark 3–4).
3. Lift pork out of the stock and bring to the boil and skim scum from the surface.
Add lettuce, dill, parsley and green part of spring onion.
4. Simmer until tender, return pork to the pot and remove from the heat.
Allow to cool for 5 minutes.
5. In a blender, blitz eggs and lemon juice until fluffy.
Add egg and lemon mix into braise.
6. Being careful not to scramble mixture, stir until sauce begins to thicken.
Add butter and stir until dissolved.
7. Adjust seasoning to taste.

I thank my grandparents and great grandparents for who they were. They were the pioneers, the creators and the visionaries. Through war and hardship they battled on and conquered.

Melitzana
Eggplant (aubergine) and tomato bake

Serves 4

Ingredients
4 medium eggplants (aubergines)
100ml (3½fl oz) extra virgin olive oil
2 brown onions, diced
200ml (7fl oz) extra virgin olive oil
4 cloves garlic, sliced
1 teaspoon ground cumin
1 teaspoon dried oregano
1 cup tinned chopped tomatoes
3 tablespoons parsley, shredded
Salt, to taste
Black pepper, to taste
300ml (10fl oz) water

Method
1. Slice eggplant in half lengthways and score. Rub flesh with olive oil and roast
at 200°C (400°F, Gas Mark 6) until almost cooked.
2. Once cool enough to handle, scoop out half the flesh, reserving shells.
3. Sauté onion in olive oil until tender. Add garlic, cumin, oregano and reserved eggplant
flesh. Cook for 2 minutes.
4. Stir in chopped tomato and parsley. Season mixture well with salt and black pepper.
5. Place eggplant shells into a tray and fill with mixture
Add water to cover bottom of tray and bake at 200°C (400°F, Gas Mark 6)
for 20 minutes.

I love my kitchen.
It's my sanity.
It's where I am
comfortable and at
peace. It allows
me to express myself
without boundaries.

Hirino yiouvetsi
Braised pork, kritharaki and feta

Serves 4

Ingredients
100ml (3½fl oz) extra virgin olive oil
1kg (2.2lb) pork shoulder, diced
2 brown onions, sliced
2 cloves garlic, peeled and finely sliced
1 cinnamon stick
500g (17½oz) crushed tomatoes
Chicken stock to cover by 3cm
500g (17½oz) kritharaki (rice shaped) pasta, rinsed
200g (6½oz) feta (I use Dodoni), crumbled
40g (1½oz) butter
Salt, to season
Kefalograviera cheese, shaved

Method
1. Heat a heavy based pot until smoking. Add half the olive oil and pork and cook until completely browned. Remove meat and set aside.
2. Add remaining olive oil and sweat onions and garlic until soft.
3. Add pork, cinnamon, tomatoes and chicken stock.
Cover and braise in oven at 170°C (220°F, Gas Mark 2) for 2 hours until pork is tender.
4. Stir in kritharaki pasta, kefalograviera cheese and bake for a further 20 minutes.
5. Remove from the oven and stir in feta and butter. Season with salt.
6. Serve topped with kefalograviera shavings.

Notes: Kefalograviera is one of the newer Greek cheeses. The taste of this hard cheese is salty, and has similar characteristics of pelorinder and even parmesan.
It is made from sheep's milk.
Kefalograviera is sold in wheels or wedges. It has a light brown rind.
It can be found at Greek or Mediterranean markets

Rabbit Stifado

Serves 4

Ingredients

250ml (8fl oz) extra virgin olive oil
1 whole rabbit cut into pieces (back legs, front legs, ribs, back)
8 medium brown onions cut into quarters
5 cloves garlic, sliced
1 tablespoon tomato paste
400ml (13½fl oz) dry red wine
250g tin (8oz) crushed tomatoes
Water, to cover
2 cinnamon sticks
2 tablespoons dried oregano
1 bay leaf
1 orange, zest and juice
4 cloves
Salt, to taste
50g (2oz) diced butter

Method

1. In a heavy based pot heat 175ml (6fl oz) olive oil and
brown off the rabbit pieces on all sides.
2. Remove from pot, add onions and cook for 3 minutes then add garlic and remaining oil
and tomato paste. Cook for a further 2 minutes.
3. Add wine and reduce by half.
Add rabbit back to the pot with remaining ingredients and enough water to just cover.
4. Cover with lid and braise in an oven at 160°C (325°F, Gas Mark 2-3) for 2½-3 hours
until onions and rabbit are tender.
5. Remove cinnamon sticks and bay leaf.
6. Using slotted spoon, remove rabbit and onions and place in serving dish.
7. Pour juices into saucepan and reduce. Finish with diced butter.
Season and pour over rabbit.

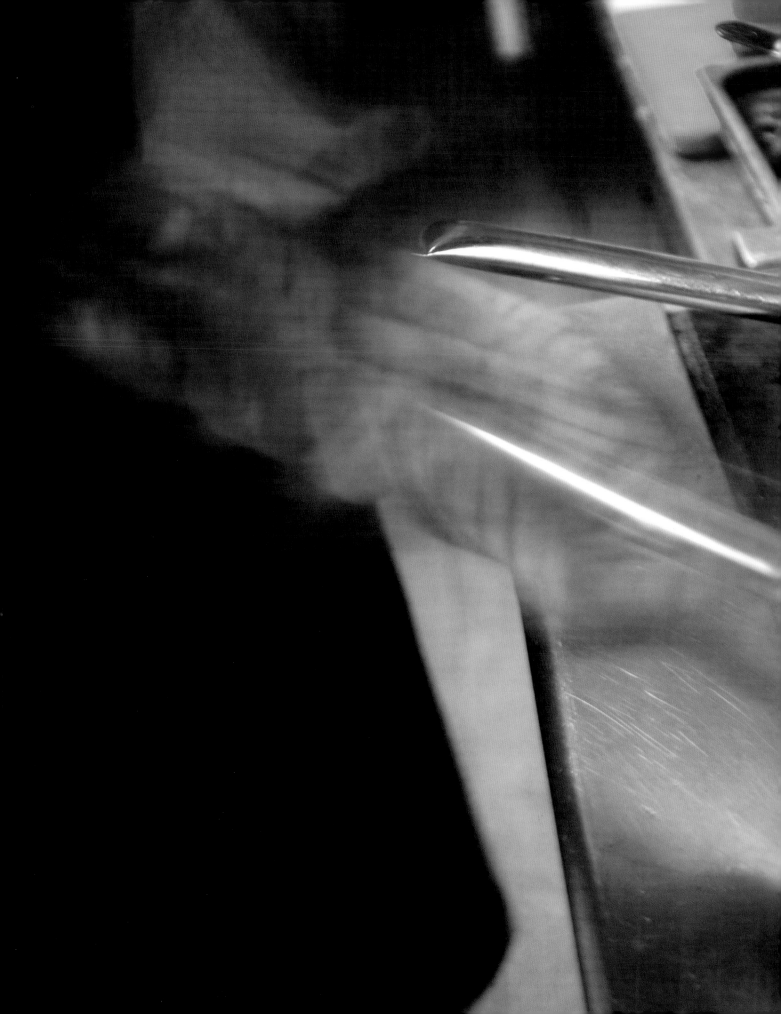

Arni kleftiko
Stolen lamb

Serves 6

Ingredients
3 large tomatoes
2 large desiree potatoes
2 medium brown onions
750g (2lb) lamb shoulder, boned
400ml (14fl oz) chicken stock
5 cloves garlic, sliced
300g (10½oz) feta (I use Dodoni), crumbled
4 thick slices stale sourdough/ciabatta bread
1 tablespoon rosemary, chopped
1 tablespoon thyme, chopped
1 tablespoon dried mint
5 tablespoons extra virgin olive oil
3 tablespoons lemon juice
1 tablespoon salt

Method
1. Dice tomatoes, potatoes, onions, bread and lamb into 2cm (1in) cubes.
2. Heat a heavy based pot and add olive oil and brown the lamb and the onions.
3. Cook until onions are soft. Add dried mint, thyme, rosemary and garlic. Cook for a further minute and then add to casserole dish.
4. Add chicken stock, and cover and braise for 2 hours at 160°C (320°F).
5. Mix all remaining ingredients together in a large bowl until well combined and pour this mixture over the lamb and bake uncovered for a further 45 minutes until the potatoes are cooked.
6. Drizzle with extra virgin olive oil and serve.

In all my kitchens I expect 100 per cent, no more, no less. When I go to my friends or families house I expect nothing more than great company and lots of love. I would never expect or criticise. I am thankful and happy.

Chicken livers with saffron-braised onions

Serves 6

Ingredients
1kg (2.2lb) chicken liver
300ml (10fl oz) full-cream milk
500g (17½oz) baby onions
Pinch of saffron threads
1 clove garlic
2 sprigs lemon thyme
2 cups chicken stock
100ml (3½ fl oz) extra virgin olive oil
Salt, to taste

Method
1. Remove thin membrane from around chicken liver and any sinews.
Place chicken liver into bowl, cover with milk and cling film
and place in a fridge for 12 hours.
2. Peel baby onions, add to saucepan along with saffron, sliced garlic, thyme and stock.
Cover and gently simmer for 20 minutes.
3. Remove lid and thyme stalks and reduce stock down to glaze consistency.
4. Wash milk from livers and pat dry.
5. Brush liver with olive oil and season. Cook on hot grill making sure not to overcook.
Stir extra virgin olive oil into saffron and onions. Season and spoon over chicken liver.

Moussaka

Serves 4

Ingredients
1 onion, finely diced
2 cloves garlic, finely diced
1 tablespoon lemon thyme, chopped
1 tablespoon rosemary, chopped
300g (10½oz) lamb mince
100g (3½oz) pork mince
100g (3½oz) veal mince
2 tablespoons tomato paste
2 cinnamon quills
250g (1¾oz) crushed tomatoes
Salt, to taste
2 eggplants (aubergine), sliced 1cm (½in) thick
3 medium-sized potatoes, 1cm (½in) thick

Béchamel
100g (3½oz) butter
100g (3½oz) flour
600ml (25fl oz) milk
3 eggs, beaten
100g (3½oz) grated keflagraviera cheese

Method

Meat sauce

1. Sauté diced onion, garlic, lemon thyme and rosemary until soft,
add all mince and brown.
2. Add tomato paste, cinnamon quills and crushed tomatoes reduce to a low heat
and simmer for 1 hour. Season to taste.
3. Brush eggplant and potatoes with olive oil and either grill on barbecue
or pan fry until tender.

Béchamel

1. Melt butter in a heavy based saucepan.
2. Add flour, stir on a low heat for 2 minutes.
3. Slowly add warm milk, continuously stirring until thick.
Cover with lid and allow to cool for 10 minutes.
4. Whisk in beaten eggs and keflagraviera cheese, season to taste.

Assemble

1. Oil casserole dish and lay eggplant over bottom. Then add a layer of meat sauce.
Arrange potato slices over meat sauce then cover with béchamel.
2. Bake in a preheated oven for 45 minutes at 200°C (400°F, Gas Mark 6) until golden
brown and béchamel has set.

Pastitsio

Serves 4

Ingredients
250g (1¾oz) long macaroni pasta
1 onion, finely diced
2 cloves garlic, finely diced
1 tablespoon lemon thyme, chopped
1 tablespoon rosemary, chopped
300g (10½oz) lamb mince
100g (3½oz) pork mince
100g (3½oz) veal mince
2 tablespoons tomato paste
2 cinnamon quills
250g (1¾oz) crushed tomatoes
Salt, to taste

Béchamel
100g (3½oz) butter
100g (3½oz) flour
800ml (27fl oz) full-cream milk
200g (6½oz) grated keflagraviera cheese
3 eggs, beaten

Method

Pasta
1. Cook pasta in boiling salted water for 8 minutes, or until al dente, strain
and toss with extra virgin olive oil and cool on tray.

Meat sauce
1. Sauté diced onion, garlic, thyme and rosemary until soft then add all mince and brown.
2. Add tomato paste, cinnamon quills and crushed tomatoes, reduce to a low
heat and simmer for 1 hour. Season to taste.

Béchamel
1. Melt butter in a heavy based saucepan.
2. Add flour, stir on low heat for 2 minutes.
2. Slowly add warm milk continuously stirring until thick.
Cover with lid and cool for 10 minutes.
3. Whisk in beaten eggs and ½ of the kefalagraviera, season to taste.

Assemble
1. Oil casserole dish, mix the other half of the grated keflagraviera through the pasta.
2. Arrange pasta on bottom of dish.
3. Cover this with meat sauce then thick layer of béchamel.
4. Bake in preheated oven at 200°C (400°F, Gas Mark 6) for 45 minutes until golden brown
and béchamel has set.

Prawn saganaki
Baked prawns (shrimp), tomato and feta

Serves 4

Ingredients
600g (28oz) whole green prawns (shrimp)
4 brown onions, sliced
250g (1¾oz) extra virgin olive oil
3 cloves garlic, sliced
1 tablespoon thyme, chopped
2 cups crushed tomatoes
1 cup water
½ bunch shredded parsley
100g (3½oz) feta (I use Dodoni), crumbled

Method
1. In a heavy based saucepan, sauté prawns in olive oil for 3 minutes.
Add sliced onion and continue to cook for further 3 minutes.
2. Add sliced garlic and thyme, cook for 2 minutes then add crushed tomatoes
and 1 cup water and simmer for 5 minutes. Season to taste.
3. Stir in shredded parsley, spoon into serving dish/bowl and sprinkle with crumbled feta.
4. Grill until golden and drizzle with extra virgin olive oil to serve.

Kokoretsi
Lamb bits cooked on the spit

Serves 4

Ingredients
250g (1¾oz) lamb sweetbreads
2 lemons
500g (17½oz) lamb liver
500g (17½oz) lamb hearts
2 lamb kidneys, halved
250g (8¾oz) sausage casings

Marinade
2 tablespoons lemon juice
½ cup olive oil
1 teaspoon dried oregano
1 teaspoon fresh thyme, chopped
1 teaspoon fresh rosemary, chopped
2 cloves garlic, crushed
1 tablespoon Dijon mustard

Method
1. Place sausage casings in bowl and cover with cold water.
2. Rinse sweetbreads, place in saucepan and cover with cold water and the juice of 1 lemon.
Slowly bring to a simmer then drain and cool.
3. Place liver, hearts and kidneys in a bowl with cold water and the juice of the other lemon.
Let soak overnight.
4. Remove the outer skin from liver and trim the larger arteries from the liver and the heart,
cut out the fatty core from the kidneys.
5. Cut all meats and sweetbreads in 3cm (1½in) pieces and place in bowl. Mix all marinade
ingredients together and cover meats. Marinade for a minimum of 4 hours.
6. Thread all the meats, alternating, onto a skewer. Drain and rinse sausage casing then
while someone else is rotating spit rod, wind the sausage casing around the offal
tucking ends into meat until finished.
7. Cook slowly on rotisserie for two hours, basting frequently,
remove from rod and serve.

My Mum's Greek
Cypriot Heart

Koupes
Cypriot pies

Serves 4

Ingredients
Dough
2 cups fine burghul (cracked wheat)
1½ cups boiling water
½ teaspoon salt
½ cup plain flour

Filling
50ml (1¾fl oz) olive oil
250g (1¾oz) lamb or beef mince
1 large onion, finely diced
½ teaspoon cinnamon powder
½ cup almonds, toasted and coarsely chopped
½ cup parsley, finely diced
Salt and pepper, to taste

Method
1. To make dough, put burghul in a bowl and add boiling water and salt.
Stir well, cover and leave for 2 hours.
2. In a hot pan, add olive oil and mince meat. Brown meat until all liquid has evaporated,
then add onion and continue to sweat. Add cinnamon powder, toasted almonds, parsley, salt
and pepper to taste. Cool mix down and reserve.
3. Knead burghal, flour and salt well to form coarse textured dough and rest for 2 hours.
Take a 50g piece of burghal dough, moisten your hands with olive oil.
Place dough in hands and flatten to make an oval shape.
4. Place 1 tablespoon of meat mixture and fold sides together to
form the shape of a small oval-shaped ball.
Fry in vegetable oil, at 180°C until golden brown on all sides.
5. Drain on a paper towel.
Serve hot with lemon and salt to taste.

My Mum's Greek Cypriot Heart

TraHana
Cypriot Easter soup

Serves 4

Ingredients

Trahana base
4 litres (8½ pints) full-cream milk
2 tablespoons table salt
500g (17½oz) thick yoghurt
4 cloves garlic
2kg (4.4lb) cracked wheat

Trahana soup
6 cups chicken stock
1 cup haloumi, diced
2 cups trahana base [see next page]
2 eggs
½ cup fresh lemon juice
Salt and pepper to taste

Make the trahana base

1. In a large pot add 2 litres (4 pints) milk and salt and stir until it reaches a boil.
Let it cool down, then add yoghurt and stir in until it dissolves.
2. Pour liquid in a large jar (5 litres/10½ pints).
After three days add 500ml (16fl oz) milk and stir thoroughly.
Use the same method until all milk is finished. Rest for another 3 days.
3. In a large pot, place sour milk and garlic and bring to the boil. When garlic is soft add
the cracked wheat and keep stirring until it becomes a thick paste.
4. The next day, wrap paste in a clean tablecloth to dry preferably outside in the sun.
Keep it covered in the fridge for 4–5 days.
5. When dry, place in a glass jar ready to use.

Method

1. Soak trahana base in cold water for one hour, drain and put in a
pot which contains chicken stock.
2. Stir on a low heat until it becomes a thick soup.
Take off heat.
3. In a bowl add eggs and lemon juice and whisk thoroughly until frothy.
4. Add to pot with trahana liquid and slowly keep stirring, then add the
diced haloumi, add salt and pepper to taste and leave to rest for 10 minutes. Eat!

Keftethes
Greek meatballs

Ingredients
1kg (2.2lb) beef mince
2 whole eggs
4 slices stale bread, remove crust
1 large potato, grated and squeezed to remove liquid
1 large onion, grated
½ cup flat leaf parsley, chopped
1 teaspoon dry mint
1 teaspoon salt
½ teaspoon black pepper
1 cup plain flour, plus extra to roll meatballs in
Lemon, to serve

Method
1. Mix all ingredients together and refrigerate for 1 hour.
2. With moistened hands shape into small balls, roll in flour.
3. Fry meatballs in hot oil until brown on all sides.
4. Remove from fry pan and let drain. Add salt.
5. Serve with lemon.

TACHINOSALATA
HOMMUS

Serves 4

Ingredients
1 x 200g (6½oz) chickpeas, soaked and boiled until tender
2 large cloves garlic, crushed
3 tablespoons tahini paste
2 tablespoons olive oil
4 tablespoons fresh lemon juice
½ teaspoon cumin powder
Paprika to taste
Salt and pepper to taste

Method
1. Drain chickpeas, preserving liquid in a bowl.
2. Put chickpeas into a food processor with ½ cup of reserved liquid.
Add garlic, tahini, olive oil, lemon juice and cumin.
Blend until smooth.
3. Place in a bowl, pour a little olive oil and sprinkle with paprika.
4. Add salt and pepper to taste.
5. Serve with warm pita bread.

Whenever I am abroad, I try to find a dining experience with soul. Listening to locals is always a great start. When I was on Mykonos, they recommended a traditional Greek taverna called Kiki's. Certainly not a Greek sounding name but nevertheless it seemed interesting enough to make the effort. Kiki's is located in the region of Agios Sostis on Mykonos. No address.

The taxi drops us at the top of the hill at Agios Sostis, overlooking the most gorgeous unspoilt beach. The taxi drives off and we're left standing with no one in sight. Someone did mention that if we got stuck, we could smell our way to the taverna. This is what we do.

We find a profoundly busy Kiki's located under a tree, on the cliff edge, overlooking a secluded beach in Agios Sostis. There is a plethora of people waiting for the ultimate dining experience! As we sit on a step waiting for a table, we are offered a Mythos beer to sip and take in the amazing view...waiting is part of the journey!

The table we are shown to has the best view in the house, overlooking the secluded beach of Agios Sostis with the most amazing crystal blue water.

Only 30 people fit under the Kiki's "tree". No menus are offered, just a trusting conversation with the staff on how hungry you are! On offer was an array of fresh salads with everything cooked on a chargrill (positioned in amongst the guests). Octopus, fresh fish, pork—everything was simple, extremely tasty and exactly what Greek cuisine is all about. The smell of the chargrill, the peaceful sounds of the ocean, the view, the food; every single sense was excited. This taverna prides itself on its raw state. It was only in late 2007 that they had electricity installed!

My experience was unforgetable and I wanted to tell all my friends about this little jewel! So I asked the owner for a business card... he looked strangely at us, chuckled and replied: "No business cards here, just memories!"

Kolokotes
Pumpkin pies

Serves 4

Ingredients

Stuffing
1 large brown onion
3 cups sweet pumpkin, diced
3 tablespoons cracked wheat
3 tablespoons cornflour oil
3 tablespoons sugar
1 cup sultanas
1 teaspoon cinnamon
½ teaspoon salt
½ teaspoon black pepper
½ teaspoon cloves
½ cup olive oil

Dough
4 cups plain flour
1 teaspoon salt
½ cup cornflour oil
1 teaspoon lemon juice
½ cup water

Method

Stuffing

1. Dice and sauté brown onion and sweet pumpkin until tender and caramelised in olive oil.
2. Mix all stuffing ingredients together in a bowl, cover with cling film and refrigerate for a few hours.

Dough

1. Sift flour and mix with salt.
Make a hole in flour and pour in oil, mix well until oil is absorbed, add lemon juice and water.
2. Knead dough to become firm, cover with a cloth and leave to rest for 45 minutes.
Knead for another 5 minutes and cut into 8 equal sized balls.
3. Roll out into an even circle with approximately 15cm (6in) diameter and 3mm thick.
4. Place 1½ tablespoons of stuffing in the middle and fold to the shape of a half moon.
With a fork press edges to seal.

To cook

1. Place kolokotes on a tray lined with baking paper and bake in a hot oven (220°C, 420°F, Gas Mark 7) for 20–25 minutes or until they are golden brown. Eat!

Coriander (cilantro) salad

Serves 4

Ingredients
1 bunch coriander (cilantro)
½ bunch spring onions
2 large tomatoes
3 Lebanese cucumbers (long cucumbers)

Dressing
100ml (3½fl oz) olive oil
50ml (1¾fl oz) balsamic vinegar
Salt and pepper to taste

Method
1. Wash vegetables and herbs and drain well.
2. Chop up coriander and spring onions, cut tomatoes into small dice, peel cucumbers and cut lengthways then cut into 1cm (½in) small dice.
3. Place in a bowl and mix thoroughly.
4. Pour on dressing and mix well before serving.

My Mum's Greek Cypriot Heart

Afelia
Braised pork and coriander (cilantro)

Serves 4

Ingredients
750g (26oz) pork loin
1½ cups dry red wine
1 teaspoon salt
1 teaspoon black pepper
2 tablespoons crushed coriander (cilantro) seeds
1kg (2.2lb) small new potatoes
1 cup cornflour oil

Method
1. Cut pork into 2cm (1in) cubes.
Place in a bowl; add wine, coriander seeds, salt and black pepper.
Mix well to blend flavours, cover and refrigerate for 2 hours.
2. Peel potatoes, wash and dry with paper towel.
Crack each potato with a mallet.
3. In a large fry pan heat oil and put a lid on.
Add potatoes and fry over a high heat and brown lightly, turning potatoes frequently.
Remove and place in a bowl.
4. Drain pork, reserving marinade and in the same fry pan, fry until golden brown.
5. Add marinate to a fry pan and reduce liquid by half.
6. Add potatoes back to the pan and sprinkle with coriander seeds.
7. Add wine marinade and reduce down to a glaze consistency.
You will have to skim any scum that rises to the surface
8. Season to taste and eat.

My Mum's Greek Cypriot Heart

My father is the man of the house, the head, the last say the director and as much as my mum is the soul, my father is the strength. Never have I met a stronger man. He has gone through a lot. A lot that I don't even know about. He's had cancer twice and has been on his death bed, but he still battles on, just like the legendary Spartans.

To this day their beliefs still live on in every Hellene: to honour and protect your family, to do whatever it takes, humility, love and passion. Family is number one.

As they would say back then and as I say every morning that I wake up alive: "Molon Lave". Here we come!

Kolokassi
Pork and taro stew

Serves 4

Ingredients
1kg (2.2lb) pork loin chops
¼ cup vegetable oil
1 large onion, chopped
1½ cups thickly sliced celery
¼ cup tomato paste
1 cup water
Salt to taste
ground pepper to taste
2 cups taro
1 large lemon

Method
1. Trim pork chops leaving some fat on the meat.
2. In a deep pan, add half the oil, fry chops until brown,
remove and put on a plate to rest.
3. Reduce heat and add remaining oil, onion and celery and fry gently until onion is
translucent.
4. Dissolve tomato paste in a cup of water. Add to the pan.
Add pork, salt, pepper and cover and simmer for 30 minutes.
5. Peel and cut the taro into large dice.
6. When meat is half cooked, place in pot on top of pork and add lemon juice.
Shake pan, do not stir.
7. Add water if required, cover and let simmer for 30–45 minutes
or until taro and pork are tender. Eat.

My Mum's Greek Cypriot Heart

When my father talks, I listen. Why? Because it's respect. And I might learn something.

Mahlepi
Chilled water jelly, pistachio and rose water

Serves 4

Ingredients
6 tablespoons cornflour
5½ cups water
Rose water to taste
Sugar to taste
Pistachio powder to taste

Method
1. Dissolve cornflour in a bowl with 1 cup of water.
2. In a pot add 4½ cups of water and bring to the boil.
Add dissolved cornflour and cook for 4 minutes.
3. After 4 minutes pour cornflour mix into serving bowls. Place in fridge to cool.
4. To serve, pour rose water over and sprinkle with sugar and pistachio powder.

Shamishi
Cypriot fried custard tarts

Serves 6

Ingredients
Custard
5 cups water
1 cup fine semolina
1 cup sugar
3 tablespoons rose water
½ teaspoon powdered mastic

Dough
1kg (2.2lb) plain flour
½ cup vegetable oil, plus extra for frying
1 teaspoon salt
Icing sugar, to serve

Method

Custard
1. Heat water to just below simmer, add semolina, sugar, rose water and mastic and keep stirring on a low heat using a wooden spoon.
2. When the custard thickens, empty into a dish and leave to rest for 1 hour covered with cling film.

Dough
1. Sift flour in a large bowl and add oil and salt, rubbing with the palm of your hands.
2. Add a small amount of warm water to flour mix and keep kneading and adding water until pastry is firm and good enough to roll with a rolling pin, allow to rest for 2 hours.
3. Cut dough into 50g balls, then roll out into 2mm (80mil) thick circles.
4. Place a large tablespoon of custard in the middle and fold into a square. The cream must be fully covered with dough.
5. Add vegetable oil in fry pan and fry until light brown by turning once on each side. Place on paper towel to drain oil.
6. Sprinkle with icing sugar and eat hot.

My Mum's Greek Cypriot Heart

Glyka: Sweets

Galaktoboureko
Milk pie

Makes 12 portions

Ingredients
1100ml (38fl oz) full-cream milk
400g (15oz) castor sugar
180g (1½oz) semolina
pinch of salt
3 eggs
1 split scraped vanilla bean
10 sheets filo pastry (1 packet), halved
250g (8oz) clarified butter
20g (¾oz) unsalted butter
1 tablespoon ground cinnamon

Syrup
250g (8oz) castor sugar
200ml (7fl oz) water
zest and juice of ½ lemon

Method
1. Bring milk, sugar, vanilla bean and cinnamon to the boil in a saucepan.
2. Mix semolina and salt together then whisk quickly into milk. Continuously whisk over medium heat for 5 minutes until thick.
3. Whisk in unsalted butter then cover with grease-proof paper to prevent skin forming. When cool mix in eggs, and leave aside.
4. Butter a 350mm x 250mm (14 x 10 inches) baking dish. Lay filo pastry on chopping board then place baking dish upside down and cut filo to the shape of the dish.
5. Place 7 sheets of filo in the dish, brushing each sheet with clarified butter. Pour in custard and top with remaining sheets of filo, brushing each with clarified butter.
6. Bake at 165°C (325°F, Gas Mark 2-3) for 45 minutes until golden brown and custard is set. While baking, bring syrup ingredients to the boil and simmer for 2 minutes then strain.
7. Pour hot syrup over galaktoboureko as soon as it comes straight from the oven.
8. Leave to cool for an hour and then portion into 12 pieces. We caramelise the top with icing sugar and a blow torch for appearance but it is just as good with icing sugar and a sprinkle of cinnamon. Also can be served with poached figs.

BOUGATSA
SEMOLINA CUSTARD, FILO PASTRY

Serves 4

Ingredients
½ vanilla bean, scraped
1½ tablespoons cornflour
2 tablespoons semolina
⅓ cup castor sugar
1 egg
330ml (11fl oz) full-cream milk
1 packet of filo pastry
1 cup clarified butter
Icing sugar, to dust
Cinnamon, to dust

Method
1. Place scraped vanilla, cornflour, semolina, sugar, egg and milk into a saucepan and blitz with stick blender until smooth.
2. Cook until it becomes custard consistency.
3. Cool on a flat tray, covered with cling film to prevent a skin forming.
4. Place 4 sheets of pastry one on top of the other, brushing liberally between each layer with clarified butter.
5. Lay filo flat and divide into 6 with a knife.
Place 1 tablespoon of the mixture on each pastry sheet and tuck up the sides and pinch together at the top.
6. Bake at 180°C (350°F, Gas Mark 6) until golden brown.
Dust with icing sugar and cinnamon.

Risogalo
Rice pudding

Serves 4

Ingredients
200g (7oz) short-grain rice, washed
400ml (12fl oz) water
½ teaspoon salt
850ml (29fl oz) full-cream milk
90g (3oz) castor sugar
1 vanilla pod, scraped
40g (1½oz) cornflour
3 egg yolks
70g (2½oz) castor sugar
2 teaspoons ground cinnamon

Method
1. Place rice in a saucepan with water and salt. Bring to the boil, stir then cover with lid.
2. Drop heat to low setting for 15 minutes until liquid is absorbed.
3. Place milk, sugar and vanilla in a saucepan and bring to a simmer.
Combine both mixtures and cook over a low heat for 20 minutes, stirring from time to time.
4. Mix cornflour with enough water to make into a wet paste.
Add into mixture and simmer lightly, stirring constantly until mixture thickens.
Remove from the heat, cover with lid and allow to cool.
5. Whisk egg yolk with castor sugar till light in colour and add to the mixture.
6. Place back on the heat and cook over a gentle heat,
stirring constantly until sauce coats rice.
Serve warm, sprinkled with cinnamon.

Glyka: Sweets

ORANGE peel spoon sweet

Serves 4

Ingredients
200g (7oz) oranges, quartered and pulp removed
400g (12oz) castor sugar
300ml (10fl oz) water
1 teaspoon lemon juice

Method
1. Roll orange peel and secure with a toothpick.
2. Place in a saucepan covered with water and boil until semi soft. Drain water.
3. Place in cold water and store in refrigerator, changing water every day for 5 days.
4. Place water, orange peel and lemon juice in a small saucepan and boil until syrup consistency.
5. Remove toothpicks and store in a sterilised sealed jar.
Serve at room temperature.

Cherry visino
Cherry spoon sweet

Serves 4

Ingredients
425g (14oz) jar of black cherries, pitted
200g (7oz) castor sugar
1 vanilla bean, split
1 teaspoon lemon juice

Method
1. Strain the cherries, reserving the liquid.
2. Place liquid, lemon juice, castor sugar and vanilla bean in saucepan
and bring to the boil.
3. Once sugar has dissolved, add the cherries and cook for a further 5 minutes.
4. Allow to cool and transfer into sterilised jars.

Note:
Serve when guests arrive at your house to give them a sense of warmth and decadence.

Mastic ice-cream

Serves 4

Ingredients
500ml (16fl oz) full-cream milk
500ml (16fl oz) thick cream
125g (¾oz) castor sugar
12 egg yolks
1 teaspoon salt
125g (¾oz) castor sugar
6 drops mastic oil (or 10g (½oz) mastic beads)

Method
1. Combine milk, cream and sugar in a saucepan and bring to the boil.
2. Whisk egg yolks, salt and sugar together until light and fluffy.
3. Slowly pour hot mixture into egg mixture (whisking while adding) and return to the heat.
Cook out over a low flame until mixture coats the back of a spoon.
4. Add mastic oil and strain.
5. Churn in an ice-cream machine till set.

Note:
If not using an ice-cream machine, take a large bowl and half fill with ice.
Sprinkle with 1 cup of salt and then place a slightly smaller bowl over the ice.
Add mixture and place in a freezer and whisk every 5 minutes until thickened.
Place into air tight container and it will keep for a week.

Mastic oil is available from Greece, and every time I visit I bring back bottles for my boys.
Most good Middle Eastern delis will stock mastic beads however, and you can infuse these
into the milk and cream at the start of this recipe.

Ekmek kataifi pagoto
Baked kataifi and custard

Serves 4

Ingredients

Base
180g (6oz) kataifi pastry
50g (1½oz) pistachio nuts, toasted and crushed
50g (1¾oz) butter, clarified

Syrup
300g (10oz) castor sugar
200ml (7fl oz) water
1 cinnamon quill
1 clove
4 strips lemon peel

Custard
225g (8oz) castor sugar
2 eggs
90g (3oz) plain flour
500ml (17fl oz) full-cream milk
1 vanilla pod scraped
50g (1¾oz) butter, diced

Method
1. Pull kataifi pastry apart and spread over the base of a baking dish
(350 x 250mm/14 x 10inches). Brush with clarified butter.
2. Bake at 180°C (350°F, Gas Mark 4) for eight minutes.
3. Combine syrup ingredients and bring to the boil.
4. Strain hot syrup over pastry as soon as it comes from the oven, then sprinkle with
pistachios and leave to cool.
5. Whisk sugar and egg together until fluffy. Add flour and whisk well.
6. Bring milk and vanilla to the boil then whisk into egg mix.
Cook over a slow heat, stirring constantly with wooden spoon until thick.
Whisk in diced butter until melted.
7. Pour custard over pastry and syrup, cover with cling film and allow to set in refrigerator.
8. Cut into 8 portions and serve with cherry visino and mastic ice-cream (previous page).

Loukoumades
Greek donuts, Attiki honey

Serves 6

Ingredients
45g (1½oz) fresh yeast
685ml (23fl oz) water, tepid (blood temperature)
600g (21oz) plain flour
50g (2oz) cornflour
1 teaspoon salt
2 tablespoons castor sugar
100ml (3fl oz) Attiki honey
50g (2oz) walnuts, toasted and crushed

Method
1. Dissolve the yeast into tepid water in a large bowl that must be able
to fit into the refrigerator.
2. Sieve flour, corn flour, salt and sugar together into a large bowl. Add water.
3. Whisk the batter until smooth, scraping the edges of the bowl as you go.
4. Cover tightly with cling film and sit on bench for 10 minutes,
then place in fridge for 1 hour before using. (This will give you crisp loukoumades.)
5. Heat oil to 170°C (338°F) or until a small amount of bread sizzles when dropped in and
using either one hand or a spoon, place small amounts of mixture into the fryer.
6. Cook until golden brown and serve hot with lashings of honey and toasted walnuts.

Note:
Attiki honey is available from most good Mediterranean delis. The bees feed on thyme leaves
during the honey making process, giving a very distinct flavour.

Baklava

Serves 4

Ingredients
300g (10½oz) honey
300g (10½oz) water
300g (10½oz) castor sugar
2 cinnamon quills
1 orange, zested
½ vanilla pod, scraped
150g (5oz) pistachio nuts, chopped into small pieces
350g (12oz) walnuts, chopped into small pieces
2 tablespoons semolina
1 teaspoon ground cinnamon
½ teaspoon salt
300ml (10fl oz) extra virgin olive oil
14 sheets filo pastry (1 packet)
Cloves for studding

Method
1. Place honey, water, sugar, cinnamon quills, orange zest and vanilla into a saucepan.
Simmer for 5 minutes before straining and chilling.
2. Combine pistachios, walnuts, semolina and cinnamon and mix well.
3. Brush a baking dish (350 x 250mm/14 x 10 inches) with olive oil and lay down 7 sheets
of filo pastry, brushing between each layer.
4. Sprinkle evenly with a layer of nut mixture, top with pastry sheet, brush with olive oil.
5. Repeat this process until all the mixture is used up,
ensuring that you press between each layer to keep an even surface.
6. Top with remaining pastry sheets, brushing between each layer. Allow to set in fridge.
7. Cut baklava into 12 pieces and insert a clove in the centre of each piece.
8. Bake at 170°C (320°F, Gas Mark 2–3) until golden brown (approx 35-40 minutes)and
pour cold syrup straight over the hot baklava so it penetrates.
Leave to cool at room temperature.

Note:
Baklava is best eaten at room temperature and not from the refrigerator.

Sokolatenia flogera, metaxa syrup and passionfruit
Chocolate custard fingers

Serves 6

Ingredients

Metaxa syrup
200g (6½oz) castor sugar
100g (3½oz) honey
200ml (7fl oz) water
100ml (3½ fl oz) metaxa (brandy)
2 fresh passionfruit pulp

Flogeres
325ml (11fl oz) full-cream milk
325ml (11fl oz) thickened cream
3 egg yolks
80g (3oz) castor sugar
35g (1¼oz) semolina
Pinch salt
180g (½oz) dark chocolate (chips or grated)
1 pack of filo pastry
250ml (1¾ fl oz) butter, clarified

Method

1. Bring sugar, honey and water to the boil, reduce for 3 minutes, add metaxa and chill.
2. Bring milk and cream to a simmer.
Cream yolks and sugar with whisk, add semolina and salt
then whisk in hot milk and cream.
Add back to pot and continuously stir with wooden spoon until thick.
3. Stir in chocolate and chill mixture with layer of cling film over surface
to prevent skin forming.
4. Lay one sheet of filo pastry horizontally, brush with clarified butter
then add another sheet.
Repeat process 3 times.
5. Cut pastry in half from top to bottom, pipe mixture along bottom edge.
Start and finish 1cm from the edge.
Continue to roll pastry until mix is finished. You should have 12 fingers.
6. Bake in a hot oven, pre heated at 200°C (400°F, Gas Mark 6) until golden.
Pour cold syrup over hot flogeres.
7. Serve with passionfruit pulp and metaxa syrup.

Notes: Flogeres (uncooked) and syrup can both be made ahead of time and refrigerated.

Melomakarona
Honey walnut cookies

Makes 26-30 cookies

Ingredients
200ml (7fl oz) oil
150g sugar
100ml (3.5fl oz) freshly squeezed orange juice
40ml (1.5fl oz) brandy
400g plain flour
125g semolina
1 teaspoon baking powder
Zest of 1 orange
1 teaspoon ground cinnamon
½ teaspoon ground cloves

Syrup
2 cups water
2 cups honey
2 cups sugar
1 cinnamon stick
6 cloves, whole
2 cups chopped walnuts

Method
1. Pre-heat oven to 175°C (350°F, Gas Mark 4).
Mix all dry ingredients in a bowl until well combined.
2. Mix oil, brandy and orange juice together and then mix to dry ingredients.
3. Knead on a well-floured bench until dough becomes sticky.
4. To make biscuits take a small handful (50g, 2oz) of the dough
and roll into round discs.
5. Place on a greased tray (not too close) and chill for 30 minutes.
Then bake in a pre-heated oven for 15–20 minutes.

Syrup
1. While cookies are baking, put water, honey, sugar, cinnamon and cloves
into a pot and bring to the boil.
2. Remove scum that comes to the surface and strain.
3. Place cookies into a tray that has sides and pour hot syrup over them until submerged.
Leave for two hours.
4. Place on a wire rack to remove excess syrup and sprinkle with walnuts.

Notes: Will store in an airtight container for up to 1 week.

Mati, or the evil eye, is a belief that the envy elicited by the good luck of fortunate people may result in their misfortune.

Karithopita
Walnut syrup cake

Serves 8

Ingredients
300g (10oz) plain flour
300g (10oz) castor sugar
1 teaspoon baking powder
1 teaspoon salt
2 teaspoon ground cinnamon
150g (5oz) diced butter
350ml (12fl oz) full-cream milk
2 eggs
250g (9oz) walnuts, toasted and crushed

Syrup
250g (9oz) castor sugar
1½ cups water
250g (9oz) honey
juice of one lemon

Method
1. Preheat oven to 170°C (350°F, Gas Mark 4).
2. Place flour, castor sugar, baking powder, salt and cinnamon into blender and pulse for 5 seconds. Add diced butter and blend until there are no lumps.
3. Add the milk and eggs and blend until smooth. Add walnuts and pulse for 5 seconds.
4. Pour this mixture into a greased baking tin (200 x 200mm/8 x 8 inches) and bake in preheated oven for 30 minutes or until a skewer comes out clean.
5. Allow to cool in a tin for half an hour while you prepare syrup.
6. Pour all syrup ingredients into a saucepan and bring to the boil.
7. Score a diamond pattern into the top of the cake and pour over the hot syrup. Allow to cool so the syrup can soak into the cake.

Kourambiethes
Almond shortbread

Makes approx 24 biscuits

Ingredients
340g (12oz) unsalted butter (room temperature)
110g icing sugar
340g plain flour
1 cup toasted slivered almonds
1 vanilla pod, halved and scraped
Extra plain flour for dusting
Extra icing sugar for dusting
1 teaspoon salt

Method
1. Beat butter and icing sugar until light and fluffy.
2. Add plain flour, salt, almonds and vanilla scrapings and
stir with spoon until just combined.
3. Knead mixture on floured bench until a soft dough forms, without being sticky.
4. Divide dough into 50g (1¾oz) portions, roll into crescent shapes.
5. Space out on a lightly greased baking tray and bake in a preheated oven
at 165°C (325°F, Gas Mark 4) for 10 minutes. Turn the tray and bake for a further 10
minutes until lightly golden.
6. Remove from the oven and place on a wire rack. Dust a sheet of baking paper with icing
sugar while the biscuits are still warm (not hot) and place on paper and dust with icing until
completely covered. Allow to cool.

Notes: Store in an airtight container for up to 1 month.

weights & measurements

Oven Temperatures

100°C	very slow	200°F	Gas Mark 1
120°C	very slow	250°F	Gas Mark 1
150°C	slow	300°F	Gas Mark 2
165°C	warm	325°F	Gas Mark 2–3
180°C	moderate	350°F	Gas Mark 4
190°C	moderately hot	375°F	Gas Mark 5
200°C	moderately hot	400°F	Gas Mark 6
220°C	hot	420°F	Gas Mark 7
230°C	very hot	450°F	Gas Mark 8
250°C	very hot	485°F	Gas Mark 9

Solid Measures

Metric	Imperial
10 g	$\frac{1}{3}$ oz
15 g	$\frac{1}{2}$ oz
20 g	$\frac{2}{3}$ oz
30 g	1 oz
45 g	$1\frac{1}{2}$ oz
60 g	2 oz
100 g	$3\frac{1}{2}$ oz
125 g	4 oz
150 g	5 oz
165 g	$5\frac{1}{2}$ oz
180 g	6 oz
200 g	7 oz
250 g	8 oz
300 g	10 oz
350 g	$11\frac{1}{2}$ oz
400 g	13 oz
500 g	1 lb
750 g	$1\frac{1}{2}$ lb
1 kg	2 lb

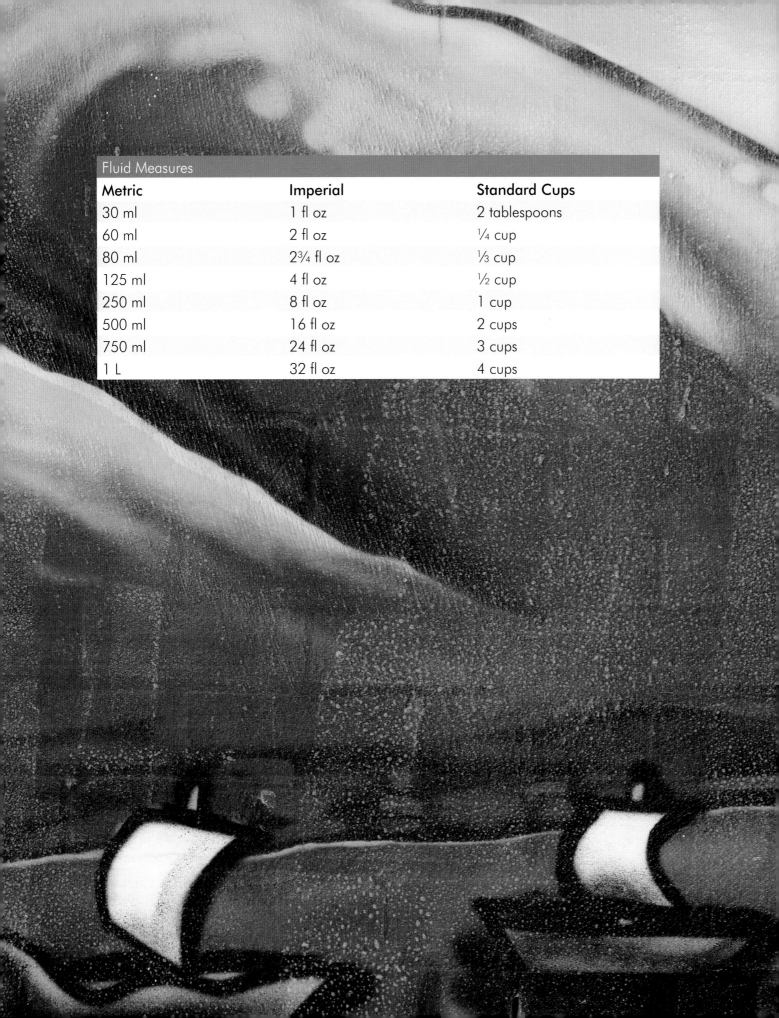

Fluid Measures

Metric	Imperial	Standard Cups
30 ml	1 fl oz	2 tablespoons
60 ml	2 fl oz	¼ cup
80 ml	2¾ fl oz	⅓ cup
125 ml	4 fl oz	½ cup
250 ml	8 fl oz	1 cup
500 ml	16 fl oz	2 cups
750 ml	24 fl oz	3 cups
1 L	32 fl oz	4 cups

Index

George Calombaris is the award-winning Chef and Director of the Hellenic Republic and The Press Club restaurants. George's cuisine has made him a much talked about chef in the international cooking circuit. He has appeared on several television programs including *Masterchef Australia*. He was voted Chef of the Year in 2008 and is regarded as one of the top 40 chefs of influence in the world.

Dean Cambray trained as a chef in some of Europe's Michelin-starred kitchens and later became one of Melbourne's highly regarded chefs, opening his own restaurant. Dean's love for photography has successfully combined to bring a new perspective to people, food and wine photography. Dean's work has been published across Australia in leading magazines, advertising campaigns and exhibitions. Dean also photographed George's first book, *The Press Club*.

This Edition published in Australia in 2015 by New Holland Publishers (Australia) Pty Ltd London • Sydney • Auckland

The Chandlery Unit 009 50 Westminster Bridge Road London SE1 7QY United Kingdom 1/66 Gibbes Street Chatswood NSW 2067 Australia 5/39 Woodside Ave Northcote Auckland 0627 New Zealand

www.newhollandpublishers.com

A record of this book is held at the British Library and the National Library of Australia
ISBN 9781742577968

Publisher: Fiona Schultz Publishing Manager: Lliane Clarke Proofreader: Bronwyn Phillips Designer: Tania Gomes Photography and styling: Dean Cambray Production Manager: Olga Dementiev Printer: Toppan Leefung Printing Ltd (China).

10 9 8 7 6 5 4 3 2 1

Hellenic Republic Restaurant 434 Lygon St Brunswick East VIC 3055, Australia +61 3 9381 1222
www.hellenicrepublic.com.au www.georgecalombaris.com.au